THE STORY BEHIND GREAT INVENTIONS

SHAWNEE LIBRARY SYSTEM

THE STORY BEHIND GREAT INVENTIONS

by Elizabeth Rider Montgomery

Drawings by Vartanian

REVISED EDITION

DODD, MEAD & COMPANY

New York

THE STORY BEHIND GREAT INVENTIONS

COPYRIGHT, 1944, BY
ELIZABETH RIDER MONTGOMERY

PRINTED IN THE UNITED STATES
OF AMERICA

Preface

IF YOUR great-great-grandparents could watch you as you go through an ordinary day's routine, they wouldn't be able to believe their eyes. The usual modern conveniences of your home—running water, electric lights, steam or gas heat—would amaze them. Your telephone and your radio would astound them. And the cars passing by on your street, and the airplanes flying overhead would frighten them out of their wits.

Your great-great-grandparents would consider this modern world of ours a world of wonders. And they would be right. Nearly everything we use in our daily lives—whether we live in the city or in the country, in the east or in the west—nearly everything we use is a marvel of invention or discovery. We cannot dress ourselves, eat a meal, go downtown or to a movie, go to school or to the library, without making use of the wonders of science and invention.

This book is written to introduce to you some of these marvels—to tell you a little of how they happened to be invented or discovered. Most inventions, in the course of their development, were the combined work of many men, and it would take forty books like this to relate their complete history. These stories are merely introductions, designed to give you a speaking acquaintance with the inventions they tell about. I have chosen, from the history of each invention, one man who was responsible for the original idea or who made an important contribution to its development. I have tried to make these men real to you by telling of their thoughts and conversations as I imagine they spoke and thought. I have tried to make their inventions clear to you by explaining a little the way they work.

If you would like to become better acquainted with great inventions, read some of the volumes listed at the end of this book.

My thanks are due to a number of people for help with this book: to Mr. John Mills of the Bell Telephone Laboratories for his valuable suggestions and criticism regarding the chapters on telephony and related subjects; to the librarians of the main Los Angeles Public Library and the North Hollywood Branch for their co-operation in locating material; to the Britannica Research Bureau for similar assistance; to several teachers and many boys and girls for reading the manuscript; to my friend, Frank Brownlee, for proofreading the completed manuscript and verifying the facts; and finally to my husband, Norman Athol Montgomery, for his patient checking of my work and his invaluable help in explaining technical facts in simple language.

Contents

	PAGE
Preface	5

PART ONE
INVENTIONS THAT HELP COMMUNICATION

PRINTING

CHAPTER
1. Printing for Poor People (*movable type—1456?*) 17
2. When Presses Roll (*rotary press—1846*) . . 22
3. "The Literary Piano" (*typewriter—1868*) . 26
4. Lines o' Type (*linotype—1885*) 32
5. Newspapers' "Single-Track Bridge" (*autoplate—1900*) 37

SOUNDS

6. The Priceless Sketchbook (*telegraph—1837*) . 47
7. Magic Messengers (*telephone—1876*) . . . 53

(The dates given are those of the patents or of the finished inventions.)

CONTENTS

CHAPTER		PAGE
8.	The Mistake That Solved a Problem (*microphone—1877*)	58
9.	Talking Tinfoil (*phonograph—1877*)	62
10.	When Wireless Became Radio (*audion tube—1906*)	67
11.	From a Whisper to a Shout (*"feedback"—1912*)	72

PICTURES

12.	The Mystery of the Chemical Cabinet (*photo developer—1839*)	81
13.	"You Press the Button—We Do the Rest" (*kodak—1888*)	85
14.	Movies Don't Move (*motion-picture projector—1894*)	90
15.	Wireless Movies (*television—1927*)	96

PART TWO

INVENTIONS THAT HELP INDUSTRY

MACHINERY

16.	"The Fire Engine" (*steam engine—1769*)	105
17.	Three Jennies (*spinning jenny—1767*)	110
18.	The Cotton Cleaner (*cotton gin—1793*)	115
19.	"Copy-Cat" (*copying lathe—1818*)	121

CONTENTS

CHAPTER	PAGE
20. From Father to Son (*reaper—1834*)	125
21. Mechanical Seamstress (*sewing machine—1845*)	129

ELECTRICITY

22. The "Impossible" Motor (*induction motor—1888*)	139
23. The Interrupted Lecture (*electric welding—1886*)	143
24. The Eye That Never Sleeps (*photoelectric cell—1887–1924*)	146
25. The Key That Became a Clue (*X-ray—1895*)	151
26. When the Furnace Door Snapped (*thermostat—1925*)	157

CHEMISTRY

27. Elastic Metal (*vulcanization—1844*)	165
28. The Match That Disappeared (*paper process—1866*)	170
29. The Struggle with Aluminum (*aluminum extraction—1886*)	174
30. Next to Diamonds (*carborundum—1893*)	179
31. The Substance That Would Not Dissolve (*bakelite—1909*)	184
32. Glass That Is Not Glass (*polaroid—1932*)	188

CONTENTS

PART THREE

INVENTIONS THAT HELP TRANSPORTATION

ON LAND

CHAPTER	PAGE
33. The Traveling Engine (*locomotive—1829*)	195
34. Bedrooms on Wheels (*Pullman sleeper—1859*)	200
35. *Stop!!* (*air-brake—1869*)	205
36. The Engine That Has No Spark Plugs (*Diesel motor—1893*)	209
37. Quantity Cars (*Ford—1892–1912*)	213
38. At the Touch of a Toe (*self-starter—1910*)	217
39. No Road Required (*caterpillar tractor—1903*)	223

IN THE WATER AND IN THE AIR

40. "Fulton's Folly" (*steamboat—1807*)	233
41. "The Fenian Ram" (*submarine—1881*)	237
42. The Third Rudder (*airplane—1903*)	241
43. The Toy That Works (*blind flying—1929*)	245
44. Anchored Airplane (*Link trainer—1928*)	249
45. Sun on Earth	253
General Bibliography	263

Illustrations

	PAGE
The rotary printing press, where the news begins rolling	15
Once elementary wireless—now high-powered radio	45
The new miracle of television	79
The "fire engine" that harnessed steam	103
Magicians of flame—the electric welders	137
Where myriad secrets of chemistry are still untold	163
The ancestor of the modern giant locomotive	193
Early challenger of the air	231
Diagram of the principal elements of the Lawrence cyclotron	254

PART ONE

INVENTIONS THAT HELP COMMUNICATION

PRINTING

The rotary printing press, where the news begins rolling

1.

Printing for Poor People

How MANY BOOKS would you read if you had to pay a hundred dollars for each one? Probably you would not read any—nor would anyone else except a few rich people. We would have no public libraries, no free textbooks for school, certainly no magazines or newspapers, for they would be just as expensive.

Five hundred years ago, a hundred dollars was a cheap price for a book. Most books sold for an amount equal to one hundred fifty to two hundred dollars. There was a very good reason for this: books were made by hand. Each page was laboriously printed and illustrated entirely by hand. Every book took months of patient work. No wonder they cost so much!

At last someone discovered that many books could be printed as easily as one, by cutting the letters out of a wooden block, and pressing the inked block on paper. But this, too, was a long, slow process. It took weeks of work to make each block, and a separate block was necessary for each page of the book. So you can see that book-making was still a difficult and expensive business until about the middle of the fifteenth century, when someone found an easier way of printing. We can not be certain who it was, but a young jewel polisher of Mainz, Germany, called John Gutenberg, is commonly believed to be the man. The circumstances of his discovery may have been something like this:

John Gutenberg was at work one evening cutting a block for a page of the Bible. For more than two weeks he had spent every evening after his jewel shop closed working on this block. It was nearly finished at last.

Anna, his wife, looked up from her sewing.

"How is the carving going, John?" she asked. "Will you finish that block tonight?"

John laid down his knife and stretched his cramped fingers.

"Yes," he nodded. "I have just two more words to cut. Then the page will be complete. How glad I will be! This carving is tiresome work."

"But think how marvelous it will be when the blocks are all finished," said his wife. "Then you can print the Gospel of St. Matthew and make as many copies as you wish."

"Yes," sighed her husband. "But this is only the first block. I must make another block for each page of the Gospel. It will take me at least a year."

He took up his knife and again set to work. But all of a sudden—the sharp knife slipped! In an instant the blade had gouged through the entire length of the nearly finished block!

"Oh!" gasped Anna. "Oh, John! How terrible! All your work ruined. Just from one slip of the knife."

John Gutenberg sat looking at the spoiled block. Bitter,

PRINTING FOR POOR PEOPLE

angry thoughts crowded through his mind. What was the use of trying to make books by block-printing, when one false move could wipe out two weeks' careful carving? He had been determined to print the Bible so that everyone could read it—even poor people who had never seen a book. But the task—long and hard at best—was hopeless if so much work could be destroyed in a moment of time.

He sat staring at the ruined block.... No. The task wasn't hopeless. He *would* accomplish it. But he must find another way of doing it.... He studied the letters that had not been in the path of the knife's blade. Beautiful even letters, carved cleanly. He must find another way of using them.

Suddenly an idea flashed into his mind. He picked up his knife and began to cut the block into pieces.

"John!" cried Anna. "Don't cut it all up! I know you are discouraged, but don't spoil *all* of the block. Perhaps you can find some method of using what is left."

"That is just what I am doing," answered John Gutenberg. "I am using what is left to learn a better way of printing. A way in which letters, once carved, can be made to print over and over again."

Wonderingly Anna laid down her work and came to look over her husband's shoulder. Then she saw that he was cutting the letters apart—cutting clear through the block, so that he made a stack of little sticks. Each little stick had a carved letter on its end.

"But I don't understand," said Anna. "How will you use these? Will you print just one letter at a time?"

"No," answered John, cutting the last of the letters

apart. "I shall put the letters together to form words, or lines, like this." He chose a few of the sticks and laid them carefully in a row. "Then I shall fasten them together and print with them." As he talked he wrapped a thread from his wife's sewing materials around the letters, fastening them securely into a solid word. It took but a moment, then, to brush ink over the letters and press them onto a piece of paper. Carefully he raised the block of letters.

Anna laughed delightedly. "Why, you have printed my name, John. It is wonderful!"

"Yes," cried John Gutenberg in great excitement. "It *is* wonderful! I have found a fast way of printing. For don't you see, Anna, by making separate letters like this I can use them over and over again. I can print thousands of books from just a few hundred letters! At last I know a way to print books easily and cheaply, so that everyone may read."

But John Gutenberg worked many years after that before his invention was successful. He had to find a better way of making movable type. The wooden letters were not durable. After a few printings, they became ink-soaked and soft. They would not print plainly. He tried making letters of lead, but that also was too soft. The pressure needed for printing flattened the letters out of shape. Then Gutenberg tried making type of iron, but iron was too hard to work with. It was almost impossible to carve letters in it. Finally, however, he found a combination of metals that worked perfectly: lead, tin and antimony.

By this time he had decided that carving letters of metal was too hard work to be practical. So he tried the scheme of

PRINTING FOR POOR PEOPLE

making a mold of the letters and pouring into it melted type metal (his combination of lead, tin and antimony). This worked well, and he found, to his delight, that he could make as many copies of a letter as he needed with very little trouble. At last he had long-lasting, clear, movable type.

The next step was a printing press with which to use the type. He took the wine press of his country as a model. A huge screw was set into the top of an upright wooden frame. Under the screw a smooth, flat board, called a platen, was fixed. The inked type, set in its frame, lay on a table. A sheet of paper was laid on the type, and then the table was pushed underneath the platen. By means of a handle the screw was lowered, forcing the platen down, thus pressing the paper firmly against the type. Then the screw was released, the paper removed from the type, and a page was printed. In this way Gutenberg was able to print, as he had said, thousands of books from just a few hundred letters. His dream of making books cheap enough for poor people to read really came true.

2.

When Presses Roll

HAVE YOU EVER seen a modern newspaper press? A huge affair it is, longer than a city block. A complicated series of endless rolls of paper and many rotary presses, it prints, folds, counts and ties into bundles thousands upon thousands of papers each hour.

How different from the small flat hand-press that Gutenberg used! Yet the flat press was used for several hundred years before rotary presses were invented. Long after men learned to operate presses by steam-power, the flat press—though too slow to keep up with the growing demand for news—was the only kind of press available. Finally, however, a member of a family of press manufacturers saw that something had to be done—and did it.

One day in 1846, the three Hoe brothers—Richard, Robert and Peter—sat in their office discussing the problems that faced their factory. Although their printing presses were the most widely used of any in America and their business was growing steadily, publishers were complaining about the slowness of the presses.

"I don't see what we can do," said Robert. "We have

improved our press over and over. It is the best on the market, by far."

"It isn't that our presses are any slower than they ever were," Peter observed. "It is just that more and more people want newspapers. The demand for news is increasing every day, and the presses can't print papers fast enough."

"What we need," said Richard, "is an entirely different kind of press—a press that will print twice as fast as our present one."

His brothers laughed. "That's easy to *say*," they scoffed. "But how can we *do* it?"

"I don't know," Richard answered, *"yet."*

That evening at home, he sat thinking about the problem. A press that would print twice as fast. It seemed impossible.

He began to visualize the press they were now making. In his mind he went over the entire process of printing, from the typesetter to the finished paper. Composing the type. Loading it in its iron frame. Laying it flat on the press. Feeding the paper, sheet by sheet, to the cylinder which rolled it against the inked type. One sheet printed. Then reach for another.... But the cylinder kept on rolling. Time was lost. Could two men feed paper to one cylinder? Was that the way to speed up printing? No, it was impossible. The frame of type had to roll back between printings to be inked. Back and forth went the type. Round and round rolled the cylinder.

Suddenly Richard stopped. His mind caught on the idea

of "rolling." Perhaps that was the way printing could be speeded up. Suppose the *type* were fastened on a cylinder instead of being flat? Both the type and the paper would roll. The cylinder of type could come in contact with the inking rollers as it turned to meet the cylinder which carried the paper. The pressure necessary to get a good impression of the type on the paper could be easily obtained by two cylinders rolling against each other—one with the type and the other with the paper. Two cylinders for rolling the paper could be used, and thus twice as many sheets could be printed in an hour as their present presses would turn out.

Richard Hoe grabbed a pencil and paper. Feverishly he set to work to figure out plans for such a press. A curved frame for the type, fastened on a large cylinder. Two smaller cylinders carrying sheets of paper—the framework of the press was easy to plan.

But then came the problem: how could *type*, which was made of metal, and would not bend, be bent to fit the curved surface of a cylinder?

For hours Richard Hoe struggled with this puzzle. But by morning he had solved it: the brass rules used between columns of a newspaper could be made wedge-shaped—wider at the top than at the bottom. In that way, the type could be made to fit the cylinder.

It was morning before he knew it. He had worked all night on his plans for the new press.

A little while later Richard greeted his brothers, waving a roll of papers at them.

"I have figured out a new 'lightning press' we can

make," he told them, "that will double the speed of printing."

His brothers stared at him, amazed. It was only yesterday afternoon they had agreed they didn't see how it could be done!

Richard, although tired and sleepy, laughed at their surprised faces and unrolled his papers to show his plans.

Thoughtfully, and with increasing belief, the brothers studied them.

"Yes," cried Robert at last, "I believe that will do it. This press will print twice as fast as our present ones. It will really be a 'lightning press'."

A few days later Richard told the editor of the *Philadelphia Public Ledger* about his plans. The journalist was enthusiastic and gave him an order for one. So immediately the three brothers began making the new rotary presses that—improved and expanded as the years have passed—have put the name of *Hoe* at the top in the printing world. When presses roll, they are usually "Hoes."

3.

"*The Literary Piano*"

CAN YOU WRITE on a typewriter? Certainly you can. Not so fast as a typist, of course, but still you can make plain, readable copy. Anyone who can read can write on a typewriter.

Today business offices, publishing houses and newspaper offices would hardly know what to do without typewriters. Yet not so many years ago the man who invented this clever machine was told that no one would ever use it. He was assured that people would not like to receive letters printed by machine instead of written artistically by hand!

Christopher Sholes was the editor of a small newspaper. In his spare time he did job printing. But he did not like job printing. It was so uninteresting. For instance, numbering the pages of the account books and check books he made was slow, monotonous work.

One day in 1866, as he sat numbering a series of tickets he had printed, his friend Sam Soule came in to walk home with him.

"Haven't you finished those tickets yet?" asked Soule.

"No," Sholes answered. "Numbering with this hand-

"THE LITERARY PIANO" 27

stamp is slow; I have to change the number after each one I print. I could write the numbers by hand just as fast."

"Yes," agreed Soule. "We ought to have machinery to do that sort of work." Sholes looked thoughtfully at the handstamp as Soule sat down to wait for him.

"Do you know, Sam," said Sholes after a minute, "I think we could make a machine that would print these numbers. Look here. We could make it like this."

Soule came to look over his shoulder as Sholes drew a rough sketch of his idea.

"Yes, sir!" cried Soule. "I believe you have an idea there. That ought to work. Let's try it."

At once the two friends started work on the stamping machine. They rented a workroom over an old mill. There, evening after evening when the day's work was over, they labored on their invention. Sometimes they worked far into the night.

Finally the stamping machine was finished. In great pride and excitement, Sholes called to the man who rented the workroom next door.

"Come in here a minute, Glidden. Come and see our invention. We have finished it."

Glidden left his own workbench and came into their room to look at the new machine.

"So that is your printing machine, is it?" he said. "Let's see how it works."

Soule proudly operated the stamping machine. It was a small, simple affair with very few keys. As the keys were pressed, one after another, it printed numbers in succession without a single mistake.

Glidden looked thoughtfully at his friends' invention. At last he said, "It's a good machine. Yes, it is a successful invention. There is no doubt about that. But wouldn't it be more useful if it printed letters and words as well as numbers? If you can make a machine that will print numbers, you can make one that will print letters. Then you could write anything."

But Sholes and Soule scarcely heard the last part of Glidden's speech. They were delighted that their invention was completed. They were pleased that he thought it a good machine. Happy and excited with their success, they did not think seriously of Glidden's suggestion.

A few weeks later, however, Sholes came across an article in *The Scientific American* that reminded him of Glidden's words. The article described a writing machine which had been invented recently. This account of "The Literary Piano," as it was called (probably because the keyboard was something like that of a piano), predicted a great future for the writing machine. It said that children of the next generation would not need to write, except to sign their names. All other writing would be done on "The Literary Piano."

Sholes read the article to Glidden and Soule.

"I knew it could be done," said Glidden. "I knew a writing machine could be made. It's too bad that fellow beat you to it."

But Sholes was studying the description of the machine given in the magazine.

"I'm not so sure he has beaten me," he said at last. "His machine is very complicated. There's a lot to get out of order. And I don't believe it would write very well. Certainly it would be very slow. I think I could make a much better writing machine."

"Well, why not try?" urged Glidden.

"Yes," agreed Soule, "why not try?"

"I will," exclaimed Sholes, "if you two will help me."

His friends agreed, and a partnership was formed. Sholes supplied most of the ideas, Glidden supplied the money, and Soule did the fine machine work. This partnership turned out to be a very good one. Sholes was clever at figuring out how to do a thing, but was not so good at carrying out his ideas. Soule, on the other hand, while not so clever at planning, could build things quickly and well, when once they were designed. And as neither of these two had any money for materials, Glidden was an indispensable partner.

The three set out to study the problem of building a writing machine. The first step was to find out everything that had been done along that line. They were amazed to discover that at least four writing machines had already been made, but none was simple enough and fast enough to be practical.

Most of these early machines were much like the toy typewriter of today: the type keys were placed in a large metal ring. In typing, this ring had to be turned until the desired letter stood over the printing space. Of course, this method was very slow. But how could they get away from it?

"The keys should be stationary," said Sholes. "The *a* should be always in the same place, so that the operator could press it without even looking at his machine. But in that case, each key should be able to make its letter hit at one certain point—*the same point for all of the letters.*"

Instantly he saw the solution.

"Why, of course," he cried. "That's easy. We will have the type bars in a *circle*. Then they can all hit in the *center* of the circle."

"Yes," said Soule, after a moment's thought. "That should work. The keys could be connected to the typebars by levers."

"As each key is pressed," Sholes went on, "a wheel could move the paper the width of a letter, so that it is ready for the next letter. Yes, I think we have the right idea. I believe we can start work on our machine."

So the work began, and after months of labor they finished their first machine. You would have laughed at it. The keyboard looked very much like that of a piano. The letters were arranged in alphabetical order (although very soon they changed to the plan that printers use of having the most-used letters nearest at hand). It printed only capital letters. The keys were invisible, and the writer could not see what he was writing until he took the paper out of the machine. Then, of course, it was too late to correct mistakes. But it worked. The writing machine really wrote. Queer as it was, this first writing machine proved to them that they had the right idea.

However, it also proved that their idea was a very difficult one to carry out. Making the paper move with each pressure of a key was hard enough, but making all type bars hit in precisely the same spot with clear, perfect letters: that was infinitely harder. They needed wheels and cams, ratchets and screws much smaller than those used in machinery in that day. It was almost impossible to do the fine accurate work that such a machine needed if it was to be practical.

So the task of building a writing machine turned out to be much longer and harder than the three friends dreamed when they formed their partnership. Soule and Glidden became discouraged and dropped out. But Sholes kept on with a new partner, Densmore. This new man had great faith in the typewriter, as Sholes now called his writing machine, but he knew that it must be almost perfect mechanically before it could be marketed successfully. So he kept at Sholes to improve it, until the inventor nearly became discouraged himself. Before he built a typewriter that was good enough to sell, Sholes built—and threw away—*fifty* machines!

At last, however, he was rewarded by having his typewriter taken over by the Remington Company, who undertook its manufacture. Typewriters were introduced into offices and homes. Slowly the world realized what a great invention it was. Although at first people hesitated to use it for fear others would be offended at receiving a typewritten letter, in a few years this prejudice was overcome. Then the typewriter became indispensable to businesses all over the country.

4.

Lines o' Type

Sometimes a big city newspaper will put out five or six different editions in one day. Have you ever wondered how they can print so many pages in one day—and especially, how they can set up the type for so many pages of printing? Or perhaps you have visited a newspaper composing room. Then you know how type is set so fast, for you have seen a linotype machine work.

The keyboard of this wonderful machine looks very much like a typewriter. But the linotype has many more keys, and they do very different work. Instead of printing a letter on paper when the operator presses a key—A, for instance—the linotype releases a matrix (a metal form) of the letter A. This matrix comes to rest in front of the machine, where it is joined by others as the operator continues pressing keys. When a whole line has been set up it is carried to a mold which is full of hot, molten type metal. There the matrices are filled with type metal, which hardens instantly. And there is a solid "line o' type" called a slug, ready to print.

Then this clever machine performs its greatest trick of all. With the pressure of a lever, each matrix—now that its work is done—goes back to its own compartment, guided by a series of teeth on its end. It is ready to be used again when needed.

Thus a linotype operator can set up about eighteen hundred lines of type during a day. So it is not surprising, after all, that newspapers are able to put out several editions in one day.

Little more than fifty years ago, however, typesetting was different. To set the type for one page of a newspaper, the typesetter had to stand for hours before his case of type. He had to pick each separate letter from its compartment and set it up in a metal "stick." And when the page was finally printed, after long, tedious work, he was not yet finished. He had still to put all the type back in the proper cases. And that seemed an endless task. In those days, a newspaper office was thankful enough to get the type set for *one* edition in a day! So modern newspapers owe a great deal to the man who invented the linotype machine.

Ottmar Mergenthaler was on his way to Washington, D. C., one day in 1884, to see some men he was working with. They were trying to invent an automatic typesetter. But they were having great difficulty. Nothing seemed to work right.

First they had tried a machine much like a typewriter that printed in lithographic ink on paper. The inked paper was then transferred to a lithographic stone for printing. But that machine did not work well. Often the copies were blurred and vague, and the process was very slow.

Next they tried pressing typewriter keys into papier-mâché to make a matrix, or form. This papier-mâché form was then filled with liquid metal to form a page of type. But that plan was not successful. The impressions of the letters in the soft papier-mâché were not clear, because each time a letter was printed, the last key pushed the previously made impressions out of shape.

Then Mergenthaler tried a third idea. He made a machine that set up printers' type, from which they made a papier-mâché matrix. He hoped that by pressing the entire page onto the papier-mâché at once he could obtain a clear-cut matrix. But that machine did not work either. The type cast from the papier-mâché form was never perfect. Even when he changed the machine so that just one line at a time was cast, still it did not work properly. Clearly, papier-mâché would never be satisfactory for their purpose. Something else must be used.

As Mergenthaler was riding on the train toward Washington that day, he was very much discouraged. He could see no way to solve the problem of the automatic typesetter. However, he had no thought of giving up. He was determined to work it out successfully. He had built many clever machines during his years of working in an electrical instrument shop, and he was sure this machine could be made practical. But as yet he didn't see how.

"The idea of casting type as it is needed is good," he thought. "Have a machine that assembles matrices instead of type, and then cast type from them. But for that kind of machine we should have brass matrices, and they are far too expensive. Two dollars each! And we would need thousands to print any kind of a newspaper at all! We could never afford brass matrices."

Gloomily he looked out of the window. The train was nearing Washington.

"If we didn't need so *many* matrices," Mergenthaler's thoughts went on. "If as soon as a matrix was used it could be put back and used over again. If we could do something of that sort, then metal matrices wouldn't be so expensive and we could use them . . ."

His thoughts continued around that idea as the train pulled into the Washington station. Mergenthaler reached for his bags. And then an idea popped into his head. A wonderful idea!

His machine could have boxes of separate matrices— separate letters! They could be set up in line by the operation of keys. When a whole line had been set up, the faces of the matrices could be filled with molten type metal. Type metal hardens instantly, so the matrices could be sent immediately back to the boxes where they belonged, to be used again. Each matrix could have a series of teeth on one edge—each letter would have a different combination. The matrices would ride on rails which would end at different boxes, dropping each letter into a certain compartment. The line of type just cast could be set up ready to print from when enough lines were made.

"That's it!" cried Mergenthaler. "That's the solution. It will work. I *know* it will work. We won't have to have so many matrices, because a few can be used over and over. So we can afford to use brass ones after all. Why didn't we think of it before?"

Grabbing his bags in great excitement, he hurried off the train to meet his partners. He could scarcely wait to tell them that their problem was solved. He could now make a successful typesetter.

And he was right. The problem *was* solved. Of course they made several machines before they built one which worked perfectly. But the idea that flashed into Mergenthaler's head as the train pulled into the Washington station proved to be one of the greatest ideas of the times. By setting up separate matrices and then casting a line of type from them, Mergenthaler's linotype has taken the work out of typesetting. It has revolutionized printing.

5.

Newspapers' "Single-Track Bridge"

EVEN WITH linotypes to speed typesetting and great rotary presses to speed printing, newspapers could not be put out fast enough to meet the demand. It was not that the presses were too slow. It was only that the stereotypers could not supply the presses with printing plates quickly enough.

Newspaper publishers had found that by making stereotype plates of a page of type, several presses could be printing the same page at the same time, thus cutting down immensely the time required for printing.

A stereotype is a mass of type in the form of a single metal plate. To make it, the form of type (many lines cast in the linotype and fastened together in a frame) is covered with a "flong," made of layers of blotting and tissue paper. The flong is pressed against the type surface, so that an impression of the type is made in the damp, soft material. The flong is dried on the type and then removed. It is now called a matrix—a mold into which the liquid type metal is poured. When the metal is partly cooled, the matrix is removed and the stereotype curved to fit the cylinder of the press.

When all of this work had to be done by hand—as it did until the beginning of the twentieth century—it was no wonder the stereotyping department slowed up the printing of newspapers. Near the end of the nineteenth century, however, a young man just out of college saw that stereotyping needed some labor-saving invention to enable it to keep up with the speed of printing. And he set to work to make one.

James Gordon Bennett, the publisher of the *New York Herald*, looked at the young man who had just come into his office.

"Hello, Henry," he said, shaking hands with his caller. "Glad to see you. What can I do for you?"

Henry A. Wise Wood smiled at his father's old friend. "You can let me look over your newspaper plant, sir, if you will," he answered. "You know I've always been interested in printing, and I studied engineering in college to be able to improve printing processes. Now I'd like to study the technical side of newspaper printing, and as your paper is one of the biggest and best, I'd like to study it here."

"Why, certainly, Henry," agreed Bennett. "Make yourself at home here at the *Herald*. Go anywhere you like. Study our plant as much as you wish. Perhaps you can find some way to enable us to print our paper faster. We are always slower than we'd like to be."

So Henry Wood began his study of the *Herald* offices.

NEWSPAPERS' "SINGLE-TRACK BRIDGE"   39

He soon found that the manufacture of newspapers involved three mechanical departments. First was the composing room, where type was set. Second was the stereotype room, where many printing plates were cast from one form of type, thus multiplying the printing capacity of the type. And third was the pressroom where the paper was printed.

In the composing room, work had been speeded up by substituting the linotype and monotype machines for hand labor. In the pressroom, giant rotary presses had taken the place of hand labor, automatically turning out papers at the rate of 15,000 to 24,000 an hour. But in the stereotype room everything was still done by hand. Making the papier-mâché matrices, pouring the hot type metal, and trimming the finished plates—all was done by skilled mechanics.

Henry Wood found the stereotyping room fascinating. All that hot, slow handwork—no laborsaving machines! Something ought to be done about it. And he was the man to do it.

The *Herald* needed 400 stereotype plates for its daily edition. Although they employed a great many stereotypers, it took an hour and a half to make the plates—an hour and a half between the time the composing room finished its work and the time the presses could start rolling.

"It's like a single-track bridge," said Wood. "The stereotyping department is a single-track bridge connecting two sections of a four-track railroad. It holds up both ends of the work."

For weeks Wood haunted the stereotype department,

studying the different operations necessary in making plates by hand, for he had determined to make a machine that would do the same work.

Finally he went to Gordon Howland, the business manager of the *Herald*.

"If your stereotype plates could be made by machine, Mr. Howland," said Wood, "your printing time could be reduced by at least an hour for each edition."

"A machine for making stereotype plates!" exclaimed Howland. "But there isn't any such thing!"

"I think I could make one for you," said Wood quietly.

Howland stared at the young man in amazement. This young college graduate offering to do something that no newspaper man had ever thought possible: make a machine for turning out stereotype plates automatically!

Wood sat waiting. He had said what he had come to say.

Finally Howland asked, "What do you want me to do?"

"Give me an order for a stereotyping machine," Wood answered.

Howland consulted Bennett and the rest of the *Herald* staff. All were agreed that if such a machine were possible, it would be a great thing for the newspaper business. But they were doubtful that one could be made.

At last a contract was drawn up, in which the *Herald* agreed to accept and pay $25,000 for a stereotyping machine provided it made satisfactory plates. Wood was to bear all the cost of building the machine and get nothing if it did not work properly.

As soon as he knew he had a buyer for his invention if

he succeeded with it, Wood set to work. He fitted up a laboratory for experimentation, and hired machinists to help him. He told no one what he was trying to do.

Henry A. Wise Wood worked for five years before he made his first successful autoplate, as the stereotyping machine was called. When in 1900 he was certain it was absolutely practical he called Mr. Howland to come and see it.

Howland was fascinated by the autoplate. It was really two machines. The first one covered the form of type with a flong, then with a blanket and a sheet of rubber. The whole thing was then passed through a mangle press to stamp an accurate cast of the original type in the soft papier-mâché flong. The flong was then placed in a matrix dryer for about two minutes where it was shaped to fit the press cylinder and dried. Then it went to the mold box of the autoplate, and was filled with molten metal pumped from a large metal pot. The matrix stayed there for about 13 seconds, being partly cooled by a system of water circulation. The plate was then removed from the matrix and sent to the second machine, in which rough edges were trimmed off so that it was ready to be used. Thus the autoplate turned out, automatically, four stereotype plates a minute, ready to print from. It was a really wonderful machine!

"But what about the stereotype mechanics that work for us?" asked Howland. "This machine will take their places. What if they make trouble about losing their jobs when this autoplate is installed at the *Herald*? There has been a lot of trouble lately over laborsaving inventions."

Wood had been thinking of that all along. That was the reason he had worked in secret: he did not want his machinery broken up by angry workmen who feared it would take their jobs.

So Wood offered to see if he could avoid trouble with the workmen. He invited a committee from the stereotypers' union to inspect his autoplate. Then he explained to them that, while some workers always lost their jobs when any laborsaving invention was made, eventually such an invention made more jobs. He assured them they would be better off in the long run.

At first the men were doubtful, but finally they agreed not to make trouble. And as the years passed, the doubling and trebling of newspaper circulation, with the increased need of men to operate machines, proved that Wood was right. His autoplate saved mechanics the hot, hard work of making stereotype plates and eventually made better jobs for them.

Thus Wood removed the bottleneck of the newspaper business—or as he put it, "the single-track bridge of the four-track railroad," enabling newspaper production to work at top speed in all three of its departments.

SOUNDS

Once elementary wireless—now high-powered radio

6.

The Priceless Sketchbook

TODAY YOU CAN send a telegram to someone on the other side of the country, and the message will be delivered to that person in less than half an hour. You can send a message to someone on the other side of the world, and it will be delivered in a very short while.

A hundred years ago the telegraph was just a dream in the minds of a few men who were experimenting with electricity. But it was left for an artist—not an electrician—to make the dream come true.

The packet ship *Sully* was docking in New York in the fall of 1832 after her long, slow trip from France. On the pier, in the crowd that was meeting the ship, were two brothers. They had come to meet a third brother, Samuel Finley Breese Morse, who was an artist of growing reputation.

"I see him," cried one brother, waving to a man standing at the rail of the boat. "See, he is waving his sketchbook."

"Yes," laughed the other. "I suppose that notebook is the most important thing Finley brought home with him. No doubt he has it crammed with sketches for new pictures."

"After these years of studying abroad," agreed the first, "he will have some great ideas. Finley will be the foremost American painter before long."

Impatiently the two waited for this returning brother to land. They were anxious to see him after his long absence. And they were eager to hear about his travels and his studies. Finley always had so much of interest to tell after a trip abroad. To hear him talk was almost as good as traveling oneself.

At last the brothers saw Finley coming toward them.

"I have something to show you," he cried, the moment he came within hearing distance. "Just wait till you see." He waved his artist's sketchbook that he still held in his hand.

Richard Morse laughed. "Hello, Finley. It's good to see you again. So you have a new idea for the great American picture, have you?"

"No," replied Finley, shaking hands with his brothers. "Not a picture. It is an invention! A really great invention! And I have the whole plan right here in my notebook, as plain as A.B.C."

His brothers looked at each other and smiled. Finley was always so enthusiastic about things. That was one of his greatest charms.

"But tell us," said Richard, as they went to claim the traveler's trunks. "Tell us about your studies. And the people you met. And the things you saw."

"Oh," said Finley. "My studies were fine. I learned a lot. Met a lot of interesting people. But all that can wait.

THE PRICELESS SKETCHBOOK 49

I want to tell you about something important: this invention of mine.

"You see," he went on, "there was a man on board ship, a Dr. Jackson, who was interested in electricity. He had an electromagnet, and he told us about some electrical experiments he had seen in Europe. He said an electric current passes instantaneously over wire of any length. *And it can be made visible at any point!*"

Finley stopped impressively, and looked at his brothers. But they only looked at each other blankly. Why was Finley so excited over a thing like that?

"Don't you see," urged Finley, "the presence of the electric current can be shown by breaking the circuit. So we can send *messages* by electricity! We can send *messages over wires!*"

Still his brothers looked puzzled, so Morse set out to explain his idea from the beginning.

"You know, don't you, that an electromagnet (a coil of wire in the shape of a horseshoe) will lose its magnetism if the current is broken?"

His brothers nodded. They understood that.

"You know, too," Morse went on, "that an electromagnet can be made to lift and drop heavy iron bars, by making and breaking the current. When the current flows through, it will lift the bars; when the current is cut off, it will drop them."

Again his brothers nodded.

"And you know that an electric current can be sent through wires of great length."

Yes, the Morse brothers knew that.

"Well, then," Finley went on, "if a current can be sent a long way, and if (by making and breaking the current) an electromagnet can be made to lift and drop an iron bar, we can send *messages* over wires by means of clicks of the iron bar, if nothing else. Messages can be transmitted *instantly* by electricity! I realized it as soon as Dr. Jackson spoke. Immediately I saw how an instrument could be made that would do it. I made drawings in my sketchbook that very night. All the rest of the six-week trip I could think of nothing else. And I have the whole plan worked out—even a sort of code to use in sending messages. It is all right here in my sketchbook. I wouldn't take a thousand dollars for this little book."

As soon as the three men were seated in the carriage, the artist, who had now turned inventor, opened his notebook.

"See," he said, "here is the apparatus I shall make. My machine is going to write down messages as they are received, instead of just clicking the signals out."

The others studied the queer drawings as Morse explained them.

"This, you see, is the sender." He pointed to a lever which was fastened in the middle over a board. At one end of the lever a curved wire hung over two little cups. On the other end was a small weight. "These little cups," explained Morse, "are full of mercury. When the lever is pressed down, the wire drops into the mercury and completes an electric circuit, because these cups are wired to a battery and an electromagnet. When the key is raised, the circuit is broken. That, you see, is my make-and-break current that sends the signals.

"And this"—Morse pointed to another drawing—"this is the receiver. Here is the electromagnet that attracts and releases a bar of iron, with the flowing and stopping of the current. When the current passes through it, the magnet makes this pendulum move, and the pencil on the bottom of the pendulum makes marks. When the current is on for just an instant, the pencil makes a very short mark, like a dot. When it is on for several instants, the pencil makes a longer mark. Thus a message can be sent in code by means of long and short marks."

Finley Morse stopped and looked at his brothers. There was no doubt that they were interested now. And, yes, they were beginning to understand his idea. He went on with his explanation.

"I have figured out a code that will be easy to use, I think. To send a message, I would tap this key on the sender, using long and short taps according to my code. The taps at my end of the wire that open and close the circuit would make lines and points at the other end of the wire, by means of that pencil. Then the lines and dots could be translated by using my code. Simple, isn't it?"

His brothers did not agree that it was simple. But they were convinced that it was wonderful—that their brother's telegraph would be a really great invention.

"Undoubtedly," they agreed, "this notebook of Finley's is going to be of far more value to our country than if it were filled with artist's drawings. No wonder he says he wouldn't take a thousand dollars for it. He ought to say he wouldn't take a *million!* That sketchbook is priceless."

And they were certainly right. The invention of the telegraph, which was based on those drawings made on the packet ship *Sully* as it crossed the ocean, brought the far corners of our big country together, and made possible a strong government that could keep in touch with every part of the nation.

7.

Magic Messengers

OF COURSE you have used a telephone many times. It is very simple, isn't it? You just lift the receiver from the hook, give the number you are calling to the operator (or dial it) and in a few seconds you hear, as plainly as if you were in the same room together, the voice of the person at the other end of the line. Even if that person is across the country from you, the voice is perfectly clear. It is almost like magic.

We could hardly get along without the telephone today. It makes life more pleasant for us: we can talk to our friends and families wherever they are. It makes life easier for us: we can order from the butcher, the grocer, and the department stores without having to make trips to their shops. And most important of all, the telephone actually makes life safer for us: we can get a doctor or a policeman or a fire engine in a hurry, just by lifting the telephone from its hook.

Yet less than a hundred years ago no one had ever heard of a telephone. The idea of talking over wires was considered utterly fantastic. Even after a young teacher of speech had proved that it could be done, most people doubted that his invention would ever be of any value to the world. They thought it was just a magic toy!

In an attic room one evening in June of 1875, Alexander Graham Bell, who was a teacher turned inventor, sat at his workbench connecting three telegraph instruments to a single wire. This was a new invention of his which he called the multiple, or harmonic telegraph, by means of which he could send many messages over one wire. Each sending instrument and its receiver were tuned to a certain musical sound. Each pair of instruments had a different pitch, so that several messages could be sent at once over one wire without being confused. These instruments had clockspring reeds that were vibrated by electromagnets. They had to be set very carefully; the spring of each receiver had to be tuned exactly to that of its own transmitter. Mr. Bell always did this tuning himself, before experimenting with his invention, to be certain that there would be no confusion of the signals sent.

As he sat at his workbench this evening, Mr. Bell was getting ready to tune the receiver springs of the three instruments before him. In the next room his assistant, Mr. Watson, sat at another workbench before three transmitters.

Bell completed the circuit connecting the instruments. Then he plucked the spring of the first receiver. Watson plucked the spring of the first transmitter. Mr. Bell adjusted the tuning screw until the vibrations of the two springs were exactly the same pitch. Then he turned to the next instrument, and plucked the spring of the receiver.

MAGIC MESSENGERS

In the adjoining room, Watson pressed the key of the second transmitter spring, starting it vibrating. But suddenly the vibration stopped. The spring was stuck. Watson plucked the spring again. Still it stuck. Again he tried to loosen it.

Then Watson looked up in alarm. Mr. Bell had burst into the room, his eyes staring.

"What did you do?" yelled Mr. Bell. "Don't change anything. Let me see."

"Why, I was just trying to loosen this spring," said Watson in surprise. "That contact is stuck. I just did this." Again his fingers plucked the reed of instrument A, which made a musical note with its vibration.

Bell bent over the bench listening. Then, wildly excited, he plunged through the door to his own work-bench.

"Twang it again," he cried.

Wonderingly Watson plucked the spring for the third time. And again Mr. Bell came dashing into the room, his hair standing on end, his eyes shining.

"It makes the same musical tone in there," he cried. "We sent TONE over this wire!"

Watson stared at him. Then he looked down at instrument A. "Don't you see, Mr. Watson?" cried the young inventor, impatiently. "Don't you see what it means? If we can send *tones*, we can send WORDS—VOICE—*SPEECH!* Mechanism which can transmit all the complex vibrations of one tone could do the same for any sound, even that of speech."

And Bell went whirling madly around the room in a wild dance of enthusiasm.

But slower Mr. Watson was studying the transmitter on his desk.

"Yes," he said at last, his face brightening. "I see how it is. And it's really very simple after all. The make-and-break points of that transmitter spring have become welded together, so we have a *continuous* current of electricity, instead of the make-and-break current that telegraphy uses. The current remains unbroken, while the vibrations of that strip of magnetized steel are generating a current of electricity."

He turned to Mr. Bell. "You pluck that reed," said Watson. "I want to listen."

He went into the other room to stand by the inventor's workbench. Sure enough, in a moment there came from receiver *A* a musical *ping*. He stood staring at the apparatus. Then he, too, became excited by the possibilities that little musical note suggested.

"It's true!" he. cried, running back to Mr. Bell. "We can send tones! It's true!"

"Of course it's true," laughed Bell. "And it is just as true that we can send speech. We can TALK OVER WIRES! For months I have thought it could be done. I was sure that if we could make a current of electricity change in intensity (just as the air changes in density in producing a sound) we could send speech over wires. I was certain it could be done. But I couldn't see before what kind of apparatus to use. Now I know exactly what to make."

Bell picked up a scrap of paper and a pencil and began to sketch.

MAGIC MESSENGERS

"Look, Watson," he said. "Make it like this: Mount a reed over a U-shaped electromagnet, as in our harmonic telegraph. Fasten the free end of the reed to a membrane drumhead, and put a mouthpiece over it to talk into. When the membrane is set in motion by the voice, it will make the reed vibrate over the pole of the magnet. That will set up in the circuit an undulatory current that is a copy of the waves in the air caused by the voice. I am sure that will work. It will translate sound waves into undulatory, or wavelike, currents of electricity."

It took many months of patient experimenting before Bell and Watson made a successful telephone, but their first crude instrument had the right idea: sounds entering the mouthpiece made the drumhead vibrate. This vibration sent an electric impulse along the wire to the drumhead of another instrument, making it vibrate exactly like the first one. Then the vibration became the original sound that had entered the mouthpiece. Thus, as in the modern telephone, sound waves were changed into electric waves, then back into sound waves again.

Although people were slow to accept and use the telephone after it was perfected, Alexander Graham Bell's invention is used so widely today that it is hard to imagine modern life without telephones: those little magic messengers that can carry our voices instantly to the farthest corners of the world.

8.

The Mistake That Solved a Problem

IN BELL'S FIRST TELEPHONES, the same instrument was both transmitter and receiver. It was a good receiver: Bell, a teacher of speech, knew a great deal about the mechanics of speech and consequently was able to make an effective mechanical mouth, or receiver, but it was a poor transmitter. Watson, Bell's assistant, said of those early phones: "You had only to shout the same thing three or four times over before the person at the other end of the line could understand most of what you said."

To be a faithful carrier of human speech, the telephone needed a transmitter (or microphone) as efficient as Bell's receiver, and a young dry-goods salesman was one of the men who paved the way for it.

Emile Berliner was trying to make a telephone. It was the winter following the Centennial Exposition in Philadelphia. Professor Bell's telephone had been exhibited there and had created much comment. Berliner had read about it, and he had heard it talked of, but he had never seen Bell's telephone.

THE MISTAKE THAT SOLVED A PROBLEM 59

The idea of transmitting speech took hold of his imagination. He wondered just how it was done. He wondered if he, too, could learn how to send speech over wires. And he began to experiment.

He knew very little about how Bell's telephone was made, and less about how it worked, for he did not have much knowledge of electricity. (Very few people, in fact, really understood Bell's invention at that time.) However, Berliner did know that Bell used an electromagnet to operate his transmitter.

"It seems to me," thought Berliner, "that battery current would be better for a transmitter."

So without any other definite ideas, and without much technical knowledge, he worked during all of his spare time trying to find out how to send speech over wires.

"Perhaps," thought Berliner at last, "if I attached a spring to a screw on a diaphragm, with an electric current passing across the contact, it might work. If I spoke against the spring, each vibration should force a broader surface of the spring against the diaphragm, and thereby produce electric sound waves in the current."

But this plan was not successful. He could not send speech. And he knew too little of electricity to understand why.

One evening he went to visit a friend of his, Alvin Richards, who was chief operator at the fire-alarm telegraph office.

"I'm learning telegraphy," Berliner told Richards. "I think it may help me in my telephone experiments."

"Have you tried operating a telegraph yet?" asked his friend.

"A little," Berliner answered.

"Let me hear what you can do. There's an instrument we don't use any more. Try it."

Berliner sat down and began to touch the telegraph key.

"Hold on," Richards interrupted. "That's wrong. That isn't the way to send telegraph messages. You must *press* the key down—not merely *touch* it."

"What difference does that make?" asked Berliner. "It makes a contact, doesn't it, whether I just touch it gently, or press it hard?"

"Telegraphy needs a firm contact," said Richards. "In long-distance transmission there is a lot of resistance. So you must make a *firm* contact in order to have enough current for clear reception at the other end of the line."

"Do you mean to say," exclaimed Berliner, "that when I press hard, more current passes over that contact than when I press gently?"

"That's exactly what I mean," the telegraph operator answered.

Berliner jumped up in great excitement. "Thanks!" he cried. "That's just what I needed to know. Good-bye!"

His mistake in operating the telegraph had solved his telephone problem.

Home he went as fast as he could go. He knew now how to make his microphone work. More current passes over a contact point with hard pressure, less current with light pressure. Then what he needed was a *loose contact* that would allow variableness of pressure—a contact that

THE MISTAKE THAT SOLVED A PROBLEM

would become broader as the pressure increased and would allow more current to flow across it for the same voltage.

He bought a child's toy drum, cut it in half, and used one half for his membrane. Inside he glued a small disk of wood to the drumhead, and stuck a sewing needle through it so that the point protruded through the membrane. Then from the rim of the drum he suspended a steel-ball button by a metal string, so that it hung against the point of the needle. There was his loose contact.

He wired the needle and metal string so that a current of electricity passed the contact point. When he spoke against the drumhead, the current was thrown into vibrations corresponding to the sound vibrations. These were carried over a wire to one of Bell's receivers, and the listener heard his words. When the speaking voice was louder, the contact was made firmer by the sound waves hitting it, and the words heard were therefore louder.

Thus Berliner's new battery transmitter changed an *existing* electric current into waves corresponding to sound waves, instead of having the force of the voice *produce* an electric current, as Bell's telephone did. His loose contact method, which was a brand-new idea in electricity, was the secret of his success.

Like all inventions, Berliner's microphone has been greatly improved as the years have passed, but his idea of varying resistance is still the basic plan of both the telephone transmitter and the radio microphone.

9.
Talking Tinfoil

YOU HAVE PLAYED a phonograph, of course. Perhaps you even have one of your own. It is easy to work, isn't it? You just put on a record, start the machine, lower the needle, and then sit back to listen. And out of your phonograph comes music, or stories, or speeches—whatever the sounds were that made the little grooves in the record.

We take the phonograph as a matter of course today. But years ago, before it was invented, people thought it was impossible to preserve sounds. In fact, when the inventor first thought of the idea, his helper said, "It's a crazy idea!"

A young man named Thomas Edison sat in his workshop one August day in 1877, watching a telegraph invention he was working on. He called it the telegrapher repeater. It was to be an instrument to take down telegraph messages and then repeat them later, when wanted. This instrument looked very much like our phonograph. A revolving metal plate bore a round sheet of paper. An electromagnet equipped with a needle pressed dots and dashes on the paper as the signals came through the machine over the telegraph wires. By reversing the operation these dots

TALKING TINFOIL

and dashes could be reproduced over another telegraph line as fast or as slowly as desired.

The inventor made the machine go slowly, while he studied the way it worked and looked for ways to improve it. He made it go faster—then faster still. When the plate was revolving very fast indeed, he noticed something odd: the machine made a musical sound.

"I wonder why that is," said the young man to himself. "I wonder why it makes a musical sound when it goes very fast." And he set to work to figure out the reason. He made many experiments with the instrument.

By the end of the day he thought he knew the answer. And he knew something else, too.

"I can make a machine," he said, "that will record the human voice, and reproduce it again whenever I want it to, just as this machine records and reproduces telegraph messages!"

So enthusiastic was Edison about the idea that he stopped work on the telegraph instrument to work out plans for the new machine.

A few days later he gave to his assistant—a young man named Kruesi—a drawing of the talking machine he had planned.

"Kruesi," he said, "make this."

"What's it for?" asked Kruesi.

"I want it to record talking," was the reply.

Now, although Edison had already made a number of successful inventions, the idea of a talking machine sounded impossible to Kruesi.

"It's a crazy idea!" he said. "And there is a lot of important work to be done. But I'll make this thing if you want it."

When Kruesi finished the model, he laid it on the inventor's desk. Then he stood, curious and amused, to see what would be done with it.

Edison looked carefully at the machine. Yes, it was just as he had planned it. There was a thin iron diaphragm with a sharp needle fastened to it, and a cylinder covered with tinfoil. He turned a crank that was attached to the cylinder. . . . Yes, it turned smoothly. He was ready to try out the machine. But he hesitated a moment, studying it. Was he right? Would this thing really record talking? He would speak close to the diaphragm, and the sound waves set up by his voice should make the iron diaphragm vibrate. The same vibrations should be carried through the needle, which would record them on the tinfoil as the cylinder turned. Would it work, or was it just a fantastic dream? Well, he would soon find out.

By this time everyone in the workshop had gathered around the desk to see the "crazy talking machine." They laughed and joked noisily.

The inventor leaned forward. He turned the crank steadily while he shouted into the mouthpiece:

> "Mary had a little lamb,
>   Its fleece was white as snow;
> And everywhere that Mary went
>   The lamb was sure to go."

The crank stopped turning. Everyone looked closely at

TALKING TINFOIL 65

the tinfoil-covered cylinder. There were little marks and grooves on the tinfoil. But what good were they?

"Scribbling!" laughed one of the men.

"Hen tracks!" joked another.

But Edison said nothing. He was pretty sure he would get some sounds from the "hen tracks." But he did not know whether they would be intelligible words or not. He turned back the cylinder, and adjusted a reproducing diaphragm, and again turned the crank.

The joking and laughing stopped suddenly, and the eyes of the group around the desk grew wide with wonder. For from that tinfoil-covered cylinder came a thin, small voice:

"Mary had a little lamb . . ."

Not a word of the rhyme was missing! The machine could really talk!

There was complete silence in the laboratory when the machine stopped. The workers were too amazed to speak, and Edison himself had nothing to say. His experiment was a success. He knew now he could make a talking machine.

Amid a wondering silence, Edison took off the tinfoil and put on another strip. Again he turned the crank and shouted into the mouthpiece.

Then he adjusted the machine for reproducing and again his voice came back from the tinfoil as he turned the crank.

The astonished men found their tongues.

"Whoopee!" shouted Kruesi. "He's done it! Thomas Edison has made a machine that really talks!"

"I want to try it," cried one man.

"I do, too," cried another.

"And I!"

"And I!"

One after another, amazed, excited, laughing, the men took turns shouting into the little mouthpiece, and then listening to their voices played back to them. It was a great day in the inventor's laboratory.

And it was a great day for us, too. Without it much of the music of the world would be lost to us. The music and voices of great artists—some of them far away and some no longer living—would be lost to the world. For although the phonograph has been greatly changed, and looks entirely different, it still works on the same principle as that first little machine made by Thomas A. Edison that played "Mary had a little lamb" on tinfoil.

10.

When Wireless Became Radio

COAST-TO-COAST broadcasts are a commonplace today. About half the programs you hear are national networks. Do you ever wonder, when you snap the switch of your radio and hear someone speaking from New York or California, how it is possible for that far-off voice to sound so plain?

In the early days of wireless, the farther the receiver was from the transmitter, the fainter were the signals heard, for radio waves lose their electrical energy as they travel through space. So coast-to-coast broadcasting was utterly impossible, clear reception at *any* distance was always doubtful, and only Morse code signals were transmitted—never the human voice. Before actual radio was possible, wireless needed a sensitive, delicate receiver that could pick up the faintest signals, and a means of magnifying and amplifying those faint murmurs into strong, clear sounds. And a young wireless fan supplied both those needs in one little glass bulb: the audion tube.

Late one night in the fall of 1900, Lee De Forest was experimenting, as usual, with his homemade wireless set.

He was working on his first invention, a new wireless receiver that he called the "Sponder."

On a table in the small, bare room was his precious receiver. In a closet, a few feet away, was his spark coil. The coil generated waves for which he listened in his detector on the table. He could turn the coil on and off by pulling a string.

Absorbed in testing his latest adjustment of the "Sponder," De Forest turned on the coil and listened carefully. Then with a sigh he turned it off. Not too good. He must find a better electrolyte for his receiver.

Again the young inventor pulled the string and listened to the buzzing of the coil. He reached across the table to make an adjustment in his apparatus. How dim the light was! That gas jet with its Welsbach mantle ought to give a better light. He turned off the buzzing coil, and moved the table directly under the gas jet. Now he would be able to see better.

He turned on the coil. . . . Funny. He still couldn't see very clearly. The light seemed dimmer than it had a moment ago. Bending closely over his "Sponder," he tinkered with the delicate mechanism, trying to improve the reception. At last he cut off the coil and straightened up. And strangely, at once the light was brighter!

Amazed, De Forest stared up at the Welsbach burner. Had the light been dimmer each time he turned on the coil? Was it the spark coil, then, that affected the light? With his eyes on the gas jet, he pulled the string, turning on the coil. Sure enough the light became dim. He cut off the coil and the light brightened. Again and again he pulled the string. Every time the spark coil buzzed, the gas light dimmed. Every time the coil stopped, the light blazed up again.

Dropping the string, De Forest sat thinking. If the gases around that incandescent Welsbach mantle were responsive to the sparking of the coil, might not some such gas be responsive to radio wave vibrations? In other words, perhaps a hot gas could be used as a detector of wireless signals—as a radio receiver. If that were so, it should be the most sensitive and delicate receiver yet known.

Excited by this possibility of a new kind of wireless receiver, De Forest rushed into the next room to get his friend Smythe, who was deeply interested in his radio work.

For hours the two young men experimented with the Welsbach burner, and analyzed its action. They wrote down full notes of every experiment. And when they went to bed, De Forest was sure he was on the track of an invention that would be much greater than his "Sponder."

But a few days later his dream exploded.

In the course of their experiments, De Forest had removed his entire apparatus into the closet with the spark coil, and closed the closet door. To their great disappointment, the young men found that with the door closed, the gas light was not dimmed. After trying it over and over, they were forced to conclude that the gas burner was not affected, as they had thought, by the *electric impulses* generated by the coil, but by the *sound* of its buzzing. When the door was closed, the sound could not reach the light, and it was not affected by the operation of the coil.

So De Forest went back to his experiments with his "Sponder" and tried to forget his dream of a receiver with incandescent gas.

But it would not be forgotten. It kept bobbing up in his mind throughout all of his wireless work. However, he had not time or money to investigate the idea until several years had passed.

When at last in 1906 De Forest was free to pursue his dream of a gas-heat wireless detector, he set to work on it in earnest. He soon reached the conclusion that a flame detector, on the order of the Welsbach burner, was impractical. So he tried heating gas in a closed glass tube by means of an electric filament.

There was in use at the time, in a radio detector, a sealed glass bulb called the Fleming valve. In its partial vacuum were two elements: a metal plate and a lamp filament, which was heated to a bright red by connection to a battery. De Forest utilized this tube for his purpose. He added a third element to it: a wire grid. Although very simple, this addition proved to be of tremendous value. The little wire grid placed between the heated filament and the small metal plate allowed another current path through the tube—a path from filament to grid. This was very important, because the grid, he found, could control the electron stream in the plate circuit. It acted as the throttle of a locomotive does, setting powerful currents in action, or cutting them off, as it was electrified positively or negatively.

De Forest called his three-element tube the audion. Today, scientifically improved but using the basic arrangement which he discovered, the audion can amplify the weakest of radio signals, making them perfectly clear and strong. By adding more tubes, sounds can be magnified millions of times.

So it was that radio, as we know it today, became possible—thanks to the audion tube, which is really the heart of radio.

11.

From a Whisper to a Shout

LEE DE FOREST's audion tube made radio possible. But many other inventions were necessary to give us the smooth, clear reception we get today. Perhaps the most important of these was the regenerative circuit, often called the "feedback." It was a discovery rather than an invention, and soon after young Armstrong stumbled onto it, De Forest discovered the same thing.

Edwin Howard Armstrong had turned the top room of his parents' home in Yonkers into a radio room. In it he had what his mother called "junk," and what his fellow members of the Radio Club of America called the best collection of tubes and receivers they had ever seen.

The other club members were particularly envious of Howard's antenna. In front of the house he had built a tall mast—one hundred seventy feet high—from which the wire stretched for a mile in two directions. Each of his friends thought that, if only he had that wonderful antenna and that marvelous collection of tubes, his radio reception would be much, much better. Still, the entire club admitted that Armstrong was far ahead of them all

FROM A WHISPER TO A SHOUT

in his knowledge of radio—especially of the audion tube.

When Howard Armstrong first got hold of his precious audion tube, he knew why he had been learning all he could about wireless ever since he was twelve years old: it was to prepare him for studying this remarkable invention of De Forest's that made wireless signals very much clearer. Armstrong was determined to discover the laws that governed its operation. So for more than two years he worked harder than ever on his electrical engineering course in Columbia University, and experimented at home with the audion tube, trying out new ideas that occurred to him.

One day in 1912, in working with his audion, he noticed something very odd: in the plate circuit were high frequency waves of perhaps 500,000 cycles.

"That's funny," thought young Armstrong. "There ought to be not more than 1000 cycles. According to all our textbooks, those high frequency waves ought not to be there. But they *are* there—not a doubt of it! What can it mean?"

Much excited, he tuned up the rest of the circuit so that it was resonant with those waves. Then he could hardly believe his ears. A moment before the signals had come in faintly, so that he needed his earphones to hear them. Now they were clear and strong: earphones were entirely unnecessary! The phones lay on the table, and the signals could be heard plainly all over the room.

Armstrong ran to the head of the stairs.

"Mother!" he shouted. "Mother! Come up and listen. My radio is clearer than it has ever been."

From the floor below he heard his mother say wonderingly, "Why, so it is, Howard! I can hear it down here!"

Back to his receiver Armstrong dashed to note carefully every detail of his hookup, while his mother climbed the stairs to see what had caused the miracle.

Together they sat by the crude radio, marveling as they clearly heard San Francisco, three thousand miles away, signaling to Honolulu, and the Hawaiian station answering. Often San Francisco had to repeat its messages before Honolulu understood, but Armstrong and his mother heard every signal perfectly.

When the two stations signed off, Mrs. Armstrong drew a deep breath and looked at her son.

"Howard," she said, "you've made a great discovery, whatever it is. I'm sure I have no idea, myself, what you have done. Do *you* know what has made this reception so clear?"

"I think I do, Mother," Armstrong answered. "You see, today I rearranged the plate coil and the grid coil of this tube, so that they are close together. I believe part of the energy from the plate circuit is fed back into the grid circuit of the same tube. The plate circuit energy is added to the energy already in the grid circuit. Thus the current is stronger, and the signals are built up—strengthened—regenerated. I think that is what has happened. But I'm not going to say anything about it to anyone else until I am sure it is a genuine discovery."

For two months he experimented daily, checking his theory, and at last he was confident that it was sound. He had discovered a regenerative circuit that really raised the voice of radio from a whisper to a shout.

Then Howard Armstrong asked his father for the money to take out a patent on his discovery, but Mr. Armstrong refused.

"You are too young, son," said his father, "to take up invention seriously. You must finish your education before you allow such things to take too much of your time."

Disappointed, and certain that someone else—sooner or later—would stumble onto the idea just as he had, young Armstrong looked around for another way of protecting his rights in the "feedback" circuit. Finally he made a drawing of his idea and took it to a notary to have it dated and witnessed.

And it was lucky that he did! As he had anticipated, someone else very soon learned the same principle—Lee De Forest—and Armstrong was sued for infringement of patent. Only his dated and notarized drawing proved, after many expensive lawsuits, that Armstrong was the original inventor of the regenerative circuit, which stands next to the audion tube in importance in radio history.

PICTURES

The new miracle of television

12.

The Mystery of the Chemical Cabinet

Do you have a snapshot of yourself? Remember when it was taken? Perhaps you were swimming, or playing ball, or talking or laughing. Whatever you were doing, the picture was snapped so quickly you scarcely knew when it was taken. You didn't have to stop what you were doing at all.

Today a roll of film can be exposed, developed and printed in just a few hours, with dozens of prints made of any of the pictures.

But a hundred years ago, photography was a very different matter. To have your picture taken in those days, you would have had to sit perfectly still in bright sunlight for at least *ten minutes!* Of course you would close your eyes, for open eyes could not keep from blinking for ten minutes. And after that long, tedious sitting, you could get only *one* picture. You could not have a dozen made to give to your friends. Men had not yet learned how to make prints from a negative. The plate itself, on which your image was exposed, would have been made up into the finished picture.

Those earliest photographs were called "daguerreotypes," after Louis Daguerre, who was the first man to make them. However, Daguerre did not invent the camera. It was not invented all at once, as was the phonograph. And it was not the work of one man alone, as was the autoplate. It took the work of several different men over a period of many years to perfect the camera sufficiently to make photographs of people. Daguerre was the man who discovered the last process necessary to do it.

One morning about the year 1837 Louis Daguerre went into his laboratory to resume his photographic experiments. His partner Niepce had left an exposed plate with him the night before. This morning Daguerre intended to try again to find a better way of fixing photographic images. He had already discovered that silver iodide was sensitive to light and made accurate images, but so far he was unable to fix those pictures successfully. The best method of developing yet discovered made only faint images, and those were the reverse in light and shade of the picture that was taken. In other words, they were "negatives," not "positives."

Daguerre went to his chemical cabinet and took out the plate. Then he nearly dropped it in amazement. For the plate was already developed! And the lights and shadows were the same as those of the image photographed! This was a "positive"! What could have developed it?

In great excitement, Daguerre looked inside the cabinet. As usual, there were many bottles and jars of chemicals. He checked them all over. . . . No, there was nothing new.

Daguerre studied the cabinet thoughtfully. Some one of

THE MYSTERY OF THE CHEMICAL CABINET 83

those chemicals must be the developing agent. But which one was it? He would experiment and find out.

That evening he removed just one chemical from the cabinet, and put in another exposed plate. The next morning he hurried to his laboratory and opened the cabinet. Eagerly he took out the plate. It, too, was developed. The chemical he had taken out, then, was not the developing agent.

Again that night Daguerre put a fresh plate in the chemical cupboard. At the same time he removed a second chemical. But in the morning the plate was developed. He had not yet found the right chemical.

Night after night Daguerre put another plate in the cabinet. Night after night he took out another chemical. But morning after morning it was the same story. The plate was always developed.

At last there remained in the cabinet just one more bottle.

"Surely," said Daguerre to Niepce, as he put in a fresh plate with the last bottle left in the cupboard. "Surely this last bottle contains the developing agent we are looking for. If I am right, this plate will be developed in the morning."

And sure enough, in the morning the plate was developed. The men were jubilant. They were sure they had found the chemical they were looking for.

Daguerre lost no time in trying it out on another plate. And then he was bitterly disappointed and greatly puzzled, for the chemical did not work! It had no effect on the exposed plate!

"Then how," wondered Niepce, "did the plate we put

in the cabinet last night become developed, if this chemical will not work? There was no other bottle in the cupboard. It *must* have been this one."

"Well," said Daguerre at last, "I am going to put another plate in the *empty cabinet* tonight. We will see if there is something in there that we do not know about."

So a fresh plate was put in the chemical cabinet and the door closed for the night.

In the morning the partners hurried to the cabinet. Anxiously they opened it and took out the plate. Amazed and bewildered, they looked at it, for the plate was developed, although the cupboard was empty of chemicals!

"Well, this is a mystery," said Daguerre. "We must examine this cabinet. There is something in here that we do not know about. A plate cannot develop itself."

Sure enough, on close examination, they found that on one of the shelves, some mercury had been spilled. Mercury, then, must be the developer they were looking for. Immediately Daguerre experimented with mercury vapor on exposed plates. And to his delight, he found that it really was an excellent developing agent, bringing out the lights and shadows exactly as they were in nature. He had succeeded in his search. He could now make pictures.

Although photography still had a long, hard way to go before your snapshot was possible, that spilled mercury in Daguerre's chemical cabinet gave it a big push forward, by providing the essential developing agent.

13.

"You Press the Button— We Do the Rest"

ANYONE CAN TAKE pictures nowadays. Even a small child can take very good snapshots with a fixed-focus kodak. It is no trick at all to look in the view finder, snap the shutter, and roll the film so it is ready to take another picture. On a trip, you can take all the pictures you wish without any extra baggage but a small camera and some little rolls of film.

About sixty years ago, however, taking pictures was a serious and complicated business. An amateur photographer going out for a day's trip looked like an explorer going to a trackless wilderness for a stay! He had to carry with him, not only his camera, which was a big and heavy affair, and plenty of bulky glass plates for film, but also his *darkroom!* He would set up his camera on the tripod and focus in it the image that he wanted to photograph. Then he would set up a lightproof tent for a darkroom, and inside it he would spread collodion on a glass plate, and dip the whole thing in an acid bath. With the plate, still dripping, in a holder, he would rush to put it in his camera and expose the picture. Then he had to take the plate back to his dark tent and develop it before it spoiled.

When he had finished taking the pictures he wanted, he packed up his miniature chemical laboratory and carried it home.

So you can readily believe that one had to be genuinely enthusiastic about photography to take pictures about 1880.

George Eastman was one of those people who were really enthusiastic about photography. When he went on a trip he liked to take back to his mother, who could not go with him, pictures of what he had seen. But he did not like the bulky glass plates, the complicated camera, the nuisance of carrying a darkroom around. The business of taking pictures ought to be made easier. He began to dream of making photography so simple that anyone could do it. Soon he was spending all his spare time—he was a bank clerk—experimenting with photography.

When he read of a dry-plate process, developed in England, Eastman was delighted. A dry plate would do away with the dirty and difficult wet plate. No more need of carrying collodion or acid. No more necessity of a darkroom when on a trip. The plates could be developed when one reached home.

"But," thought Eastman. "It still isn't good enough. Glass plates of any kind are hard for the amateur photographer to handle. They are heavy to carry, and they are apt to break. No, what we need is something unbreakable, something light and flexible that might roll up inside the camera. That's what I want to find."

For years Eastman worked and experimented. He started a small factory, quitting his bank job at last, and made dry plates. They were very popular, being so much easier to use than the old wet plates, and the factory did well. But all the time Eastman was experimenting with other materials besides glass, trying to find a satisfactory flexible film. And at last he found he could coat paper with a gelatin emulsion to make an excellent photographic film. Now he was ready to make a camera that anyone could use.

When his first camera was finished, in 1888, it was a little black box, nearly square. It had no tripod, for it was to be held in the hands. There were no plates to put in—not even film, for the paper film, on a roll, was already inside the camera. The roll held enough film for one hundred exposures. All the photographer would have to do was focus the desired picture in the view finder, press the button, and turn the roll to a new exposure. When the hundred pictures were taken, he would send the camera back to Eastman's factory, where the film would be developed and printed for him.

George Eastman was delighted with this little camera. He was certain it would accomplish what he had dreamed of: make photography so easy that anyone and everyone could take pictures.

When production of the new camera was under way in his factory, Eastman undertook to make up a name for it. With a pencil and a pad of paper in hand, he sat under a shaded lamp one night, thinking. In advertising, he intended to use the sentence, "You press the button—we do the rest." He believed the name for his product would be as important as all the advertising he could do, and he intended to coin a name so unusual and distinctive that it would be easily recognized and remembered—a name that would always be associated with his new, simple little camera.

How should he start? Should he take two already known words, such as *camera* and *easy*, and put parts of them together to make one word?

"No," Eastman decided. "This name shall not be made up of other words. I shall make a really *new* word."

He had always liked the letter "K." It seemed so firm and unyielding. So he put "K" down on his paper. Now what would go with "K"? At once "O" leaped into his mind, so he wrote it beside the "K."

"KO," read Eastman. "That's a good first syllable. Short and crisp. Now for a second syllable."

Eastman thought for a long time. Then he set down another "K" at a little distance from his "KO." Beginning and ending the name with "K" seemed a good idea.

It was hours before the other letters fell into place. But when at last he wrote "D" and "A" in the blank space, Eastman knew he had exactly the name he was looking for: Kodak! "Ko" sounded much like the button as it was pressed; "dak" like the click of the shutter. And the whole name was easy to say and easy to remember. Kodak! Yes, it was a good name.

As everyone knows, the Kodak served its purpose of making picture taking easy enough and cheap enough so that anyone could do it. And it soon made snapshots as common and as popular as George Eastman had hoped. Though celluloid was soon substituted for paper as film, and the film made much shorter (since it was now possible for the user to put in the film himself) the word Kodak continued to stand for easy, quick picture taking, and is known the world over for that.

14.

Movies Don't Move

ARE YOU A movie fan? Whether you are or not, you have seen many moving pictures. Perhaps you even have a small movie outfit in your home. The idea of moving pictures is as familiar to us today as the idea of dressing in the morning.

But could you explain what moving pictures are to someone who had never seen any? You would be surprised to find how difficult that is. It was a task that almost stumped one of the early inventors in the movie world—the man who took the motion out of moving pictures, so they give the impression of motion without blur or flicker.

In the early 1890's C. Francis Jenkins was a stenographer in a Washington, D. C., government office. But to him stenography was only a way of earning a living. His real interest lay in the project that he spent his evenings and holidays on: the invention of a motion-picture projector.

He could not remember when he had begun thinking of this idea. It seemed to have been in the back of his mind through his entire boyhood on the farm, and in his months of studying stenography. When he came to Mr. Kimball's office in Washington to work as a stenographer, he began to make his idea into a reality.

Like all boys of his generation, Francis Jenkins was familiar with the movie-like toy called a zoetrope. This was a circular box with a wheel inside. On the rim of the wheel a series of pictures was mounted. As the wheel revolved, the pictures flashed past a hole in the box, each picture being visible for an instant. The effect, though somewhat blurred, was that of a moving picture.

There was also the kinetoscope which Thomas A. Edison had invented. In this an endless belt of celluloid film moved over sprocket wheels. The pictures were viewed through a peep-hole, as each picture passed between the eye and a lighting device.

"But that's the wrong way to do it," said Jenkins. "The pictures should not move while they are in front of the eye. If each picture were stationary for a fraction of a second, the eye could see it clearly, without any blur or flicker. And since the eye holds an image for an instant after it sees it, we would have a clear impression of motion."

But how could pictures be moved and stopped, smoothly and accurately, fast enough to look like a continuous moving picture? That was a puzzler.

At last, after months of experimenting, Jenkins hit on the plan of making a long strip of film with little holes all along one edge. He built a projecting machine with a pegged wheel, or sprocket, that fitted into the holes of the film. This wheel, turned by an electric motor, unwound the film from its spool. Each hole in turn was engaged and the film unwound just enough to show one new picture. Almost instantly, the next hole was caught, then the next, and the next, leaving each picture stationary for a split second. While the film was moving, a shutter cut off the light, so that the eye saw only a series of still pictures, but in such quick succession that they seemed to be moving.

Since he had to make his projector and his camera, cut his film, make its holes, devise a film cement for splicing it, build his developing apparatus—in fact, everything he used he had to make—naturally the invention went slowly. But finally one night with light from an oil lamp, Jenkins actually produced the first movies in which the flicker did not hurt the eyes.

But although he had solved the technical problems of his invention, Jenkins now faced a different kind of problem: how to make some money out of it. His friends enjoyed seeing his pictures. People thought them a lot of fun. But no one wanted to buy his invention. No one with money to spare saw any value in it. What good was a picture machine, anyway? A clever toy, of course, but of no use. Why buy a thing that served no practical purpose, and hence would never make any money for its owner?

Francis Jenkins had to prove that people would pay for being entertained, and that moving pictures were really entertaining.

With the backing of a friend, Thomas Armat, he decided to take his machine to the Cotton States Exposition which was being held in Atlanta, Georgia, in 1895. It would be a good place to get his invention before the public and prove its entertainment possibilities.

MOVIES DON'T MOVE

They rented a small hall, equipped it with seats and a curtain, and set up the motion-picture apparatus. They hired the best "barker" they could find to stand outside the hall and persuade people to come in. Then Jenkins and Armat waited for a crowd to gather before they started the show.

But no crowd came. Outside, people strolled to and fro, from one exhibit to another. The barker shouted at the top of his lungs:

"Step inside, ladies and gentlemen, and see the thrill of a life-time: moving pictures. Only 25¢ to see this wonderful new invention: motion pictures. Step inside. Just 25¢."

People passing looked at him in a mildly astonished way and sauntered on. Moving pictures, indeed! Who ever heard of such a thing! What was he talking about?

The barker tried again. "Moving pictures, ladies and gentlemen. Pictures that really move before your eyes. See a lady dancing—really dancing. Come in and see the wonderful moving pictures. Only 25¢. The fourth part of a dollar."

Still no one gave him more than a puzzled glance. Why was he shouting? Of course they had seen pictures of ladies dancing. What did he mean by *motion* pictures? No one understood the idea enough to be interested in it.

At last, hoarse, perspiring, discouraged, the barker went inside where Jenkins and Armat sat in the empty hall.

"I give up," he croaked. "Nobody knows what I'm talking about. How in the world can you explain motion pictures to someone who has never seen them?"

Helplessly, the other two shook their heads. They had no suggestions to offer. The barker was right. Motion pictures have to be *seen* to be understood.

Jenkins thought about that for a minute. Then his face lighted. "Our pictures have to be *seen* to be comprehended. Then we will get people to see them without knowing what they are seeing!"

"How?" asked Armat. "If people won't come in knowing they are going to see moving pictures, why would they come in *not* knowing?"

"To rest!" cried Jenkins triumphantly. "People get tired out there on the grounds, walking from one exhibit to another. We will get them to come in and rest, and *then* show the pictures."

The others shook their heads dubiously. It probably wouldn't work. But neither had a better idea, so it was worth a try.

Again the barker went outside.

"Come in and rest, ladies and gentlemen," he shouted. "Plenty of chairs inside. Come in and cool off. Come in and rest."

Two foot-weary women paused, surprised at the unusual invitation. Then they turned in at the door and thankfully sat on the nearest chairs. Others soon followed. In a few minutes half the chairs were taken, and Jenkins decided to begin the show.

Armat put out the lights, and at once Jenkins started the projector.

Startled at the sudden darkness, the audience was even more surprised at the amazing sight that immediately

MOVIES DON'T MOVE 95

met their eyes. Pictures—quite large pictures—that ACTUALLY MOVED! A girl was whirling, bending, stepping in the figures of a dance! It was amazing! She seemed almost REAL!

When the show was over and the lights again turned on, Jenkins explained briefly to his involuntary audience what they had seen—the first real public exhibition of moving pictures.

"If you care to," he ended, "and you feel the show was worth it, we would be glad for you to leave 25¢ at the box office."

Slowly the group straggled out, talking about the wonder of pictures that moved. Most of them stopped at the box office and paid. A few hurried out, muttering that it was probably a fake.

Again the barker invited people in to rest. Again, when a sufficient number had gathered, the pictures were shown. And again the visitors was asked to pay if they thought the pictures worth it.

In this way, Jenkins proved that, once people had seen his movies and understood what they were like, they were interested in them and were willing to pay for the entertainment. So eventually he was able to sell his invention. Thomas A. Edison acquired his rights and later formed the first commercial motion-picture company.

Although movies have been vastly improved by many subsequent inventions, C. Francis Jenkins started them out in the right direction by showing how to eliminate the flicker caused by the film moving before the eyes.

15.

Wireless Movies

As soon as men learned to send sounds without wires, they immediately began to think of transmitting pictures, too, through the air. But this proved to be a much harder problem.

In sending sounds through space, it was necessary only to change each sound wave into a corresponding electrical impulse, and then change it back again at the receiving end into sound. To send a picture, however (which is a *pattern* of varying intensities of light and shade, not just a single light value) the pattern must be torn into tiny bits; then each bit of light or shade must be changed separately into an electrical impulse, changed back to light at the other end, and all of the bits put together again into the original pattern of light and shadow.

It sounds complicated, doesn't it? Well, it is just as complicated as it sounds. And that is the reason television has taken so long to develop. For even after research experts had figured out how to accomplish television, and had made apparatus that actually worked (with a whirling disk to do the "scanning" or tearing apart)—even then television was not a success because this scanning disk could not work *fast* enough. You must understand that the business of taking a picture apart—into as many as 200,000 pieces—transmitting each of these as light impulses, and reassembling the picture: all of this must be done in about *1/30 of a second!* Imagine it! We think of movies as being fast in their operation, yet they usually show only twenty-four pictures each second—slower than television, and very much simpler, since movies have only to project the pictures exactly as the camera took them—not tear them to bits and change them to electrical impulses.

If it is hard for you to *imagine* the speed necessary for television's operation, you can understand how difficult it was for the television pioneers to make apparatus that would *attain* such speed. And any speed less than thirty pictures a second would not make clear, steady pictures that the eye could enjoy.

So television, though born at about the same time as radio, was very much slower growing. And it did not grow up until a high-school boy's day dream of harnessing electrons, to make eyes for television, came true.

Philo T. Farnsworth was discouraged. Here he was, in 1925, nineteen years old, ambitious and industrious, and with a great idea—but he wasn't getting anywhere. He had tried running a radio shop, but it had failed. He had tried working in the railroad yards, but the work was too strenuous for a none-too-strong youngster. And now he had another job—such as it was: helping George Everson, who was directing a fund-raising campaign in southern Utah. What would a job like that amount to for a boy who was interested in television, not in money-raising campaigns?

Yes, Phil was discouraged. It was four years since he had come across his big idea of electronic television. Four long years, and still he had no chance of working out his idea. He had been in high school when he learned about electrons—electrons that whirl at unbelievable speeds around an atom. He had learned that, under certain conditions, these electrons will break away from their atom and go flying off into space. Almost at once he had imagined using these fast-flying electrons in television: by focusing an image through a camera lens onto a sensitized surface, electrons would be given off; by transmitting and reassembling these electrons, the image could be reproduced at some distant point. Electrons—and electrons only—were capable of the speed necessary in television.

Phil had been sure of the soundness of his plan in that long ago high-school day. And he was sure of it now. But in order to convince anyone else, he would have to make apparatus that would actually carry out his idea: he would have to show that electronic-television was practical. And he had neither the money nor the laboratory equipment for doing it. So it was no wonder he was discouraged.

"Well," said Phil to himself one day, "if I can't do anything about an electronic television system myself, I might as well let someone else try it. I'll write it up as a magazine article. At least I might make a little money out of it that way."

So he set to work to put his intricate scheme down on paper. He became so absorbed in this task that he took it to work with him to mull over in his spare time.

Soon one of his fellow workers became curious, and

WIRELESS MOVIES 99

when he learned what Phil was doing, he was amazed.

"Say," he said to Everson, their boss. "Do you know what that new fellow Farnsworth is doing? He is working out a scheme of electronic television!"

"Electronic television!" exclaimed Everson. "I never heard of such a thing. But then, I don't know much about television."

However, the idea interested Everson so much that he sent for Farnsworth and asked him to explain his plan of television. And although he did not entirely understand Phil's explanation, he did realize that the boy had a really great idea.

A few days later Everson sent for Phil again.

"I'm through with my work here in Utah," he said. "I'm going to Los Angeles now to conduct a community-chest campaign. Would you like to go with me, Farnsworth? We can find a patent attorney in Los Angeles and get your television plan patented. That is very important, young fellow, for someone else will soon steal your idea unless it is patented. Then we will see if we can find some financial backing so that you can develop your invention."

The next twenty-four hours were hectic ones for Phil Farnsworth. In that short space of time he packed his clothes, married his childhood sweetheart, and was on his way to Los Angeles with his new wife.

Within a few months he had taken out patents on his entire system of electronic television, and—thanks to George Everson's help—had secured the necessary financial backing from two Los Angeles business men. At last he was started on the long, hard, but vastly absorbing task of making apparatus to put his plan in practice. Although the television equipment used today is due to the ideas and efforts of many different men (foremost among whom is Zworykin of R.C.A.), it is based on Farnsworth's electronic system.

Modern television apparatus is very complicated. The heart of it is the iconoscope, which is a vacuum tube behind the television camera lens. The iconoscope, or "ike," is to television what the microphone, or "mike," is to radio. It picks up the scene to be televised.

Within the "ike" is a light-sensitive plate or rather thousands upon thousands of light-sensitive globules, which are really tiny photoelectric cells. As light rays strike these globules they become electrically charged with faint currents which vary according to the intensity of the light rays striking them.

The scanning of the screen is done by an electron beam that moves at incredible speed back and forth across the plate collecting the electrical charges of the tiny globules. The charges are amplified and controlled, and sent by cable to the television transmitter.

So for Philo Farnsworth, the job that he thought useless to him turned out to be just the contact he needed in order to carry out his dream of a television system without moving parts, in which electrons—moving at the speed of light itself—transmit moving pictures through the air for us to enjoy in our homes.

PART TWO

INVENTIONS THAT HELP INDUSTRY

MACHINERY

The "fire engine" that harnessed steam.

16.

The "Fire Engine"

HAVE YOU EVER watched the steam engine in a big locomotive? How fast the steam turns the wheels! The train fairly flies over the rails at a breath-taking speed. And we say to ourselves, "What a wonderful thing steam is! What a lot of work it can do!"

But long ago people did not know how powerful steam is, or how to make it work. In fact, they knew very little about it until a young Scotsman began to work on a broken steam engine—he called it a "fire engine"!

On the grounds of the University of Glasgow was a little shop where a young man worked making and repairing violins, flutes and harps. He also cleaned and mended all kinds of instruments for the university, and made and sold fishing tackle and spectacles. As you can see, this young man was a "jack-of-all-trades," and he never lacked for something to do.

One day in 1765, as he sat working on an organ, a professor from the university came in with a queer-looking, clumsy engine.

"Good morning, Jamie," said the professor. "Here is something to try your skill on."

James Watt looked up from his work. "What is it? Something else broken, Professor?"

The professor nodded. "Yes. It is a model of Newcomen's engine. It won't work."

Jamie jumped up in great excitement. "A fire engine!" he cried. "I've long been wanting to see one. I'll be glad to mend this engine, just to see what I can learn about steam. I tell you, Professor, steam could be made to do great things, if only we could find out how to use it."

Eagerly Watt examined the strange model. A piston was fitted into a cylinder. The top of the piston was fastened to a beam. At the other end of the beam was a pump rod.

Yes, he could see how it worked: water was put into the cylinder and heated, by building a fire underneath. As the water boiled, steam drove all of the air out of the cylinder. Then the steam was shut off and cold water was sprayed into the cylinder. Of course the cold water condensed the steam, and this created a vacuum in the cylinder, so that the outer air pressed the piston down. As the piston went down, the pump rod on the other end of the beam went up. Then the cylinder was again filled with steam, the piston went up, and the pump rod went down. Thus the engine was made to operate a pump.

"Well," said the professor at last, starting for the door. "Learn all you can about steam from this engine, Jamie. Perhaps you can find out how to make it run without burning so much coal. Steam engines will never be widely used, I'm afraid, for they are much too expensive to operate."

THE "FIRE ENGINE"

But James Watt scarcely heard him. He was already at work on the "fire engine."

When the steam engine was repaired, Watt filled the boiler and started a fire under it. Then he watched intently. Soon steam was formed in the cylinder and the engine began to operate. For a few minutes it worked furiously. Then the engine stopped. The water was all used up. Watt had to refill the boiler and build up the fire.

Again the engine worked well for a few minutes and then stopped. . . . Out of water. Again Watt built up the fire and refilled the boiler. . . .

After several trials, James Watt sat back and looked thoughtfully at the steam engine. The professor was right. It used far too much water and coal. It would be very expensive to run.

"But, why?" he wondered. "Why does it use so much steam? I am going to find out *why*. And then I will make a fire engine that is cheap to run."

It did not take him long to figure out why the engine used so much fuel. He soon saw that the cylinder was cooled every time cold water was sprayed into it to condense the steam. Consequently, some of the heat of the next injection of steam was lost in reheating the cylinder. If the engine was to use less steam the cylinder must be kept always hot. But how, then, could the steam be condensed to operate the pump? He could not answer that question.

During the next weeks James Watt spent all the time he could spare from his work on the puzzle of the steam engine that used too much steam. He read everything he could find about what others had tried to do with steam. He made experiment after experiment. He thought and thought, trying to figure out how to make an engine that would have a lot of power, but would use less steam. He learned a great deal about steam itself, its nature and its powers.

At last he found the solution to his problem. As he was walking one day on the university grounds an idea flashed into his mind:

"Steam could be condensed in a *separate* compartment, connected with the cylinder by a short pipe. Then the cylinder itself could be kept always hot and no steam would be wasted. Thus the engine would have more power, and use less fuel."

Greatly excited, he hurried back to his shop to try out his idea. He piped the steam out of the cylinder into a separate condenser, leaving the cylinder hot. He closed the top of the cylinder to prevent the loss of steam. Immediately he became convinced that he had the right idea. His small engine, although far from perfect, had much more power, and at the same time used much less fuel than Newcomen's engine.

But when Watt had figured out how to make his engine, that was not the end of his work; it was only the beginning. He had to make his own tools, for the tools necessary to build an efficient engine like he was planning had never yet been made. He found that it cost money to build steam engines, and that he had to build not one, but many, in order to make a successful one. So when he had spent all his own money, James Watt borrowed more and went on working.

After five long years of work, his "fire engine" was a success. Men began to see how valuable steam power could be. They began to use his engine to pump water out of flooded mines. They began to use it on trains to haul passengers and freight, and on boats. And they began to use it to operate the machinery in great factories.

So James Watt, by discovering why the little model engine used too much steam, made it possible for men to do great things with steam.

17.

Three Jennies

Suppose, when you needed a new dress or shirt, you had to wait for your mother to spin the cotton. Then you had to wait for the material to be woven. And THEN you had to wait for the garment to be cut and made! Think what a long time you would have to wait for new clothes!

Well, years and years ago children had to do just that; wait a long time for new clothes. Spinning alone took a great deal of time. For a single garment, it took many, many hours of patient spinning to prepare the yarn, before the weaving could be started. Weavers were always having to wait for the spinners to spin the yarn they needed. But at last a weaver grew tired of waiting for the spinning to be done, and he invented a faster way of spinning.

James Hargreaves sat idly by his loom one day about 1764. He was a weaver, but he could not work because he had run out of yarn. There was nothing to do but wait until his wife could spin some more yarn.

So he sat watching his wife's spinning wheel busily turning, across the room from him. How he wished she could spin faster! Oh, the wheel itself turned fast enough.

And his wife's foot, pressing the treadle, moved rapidly. And the spindle, whirling to twist the yarn, went very fast indeed. But the finished thread, wound on the bottom of the spindle, seemed to increase very, very slowly.

His wife's nimble fingers drew out a length of roving (cotton fibers twisted loosely together) and held it as the rapidly twirling spindle twisted it into fine finished yarn. Then she wound the length of yarn on the bottom of the spindle and drew out another length of roving.

James Hargreaves sighed. How he wished she could spin faster! Every hour of waiting meant less money earned from his weaving. And he had to wait so often, as now, for his wife's spinning to catch up with his weaving. Why wasn't there a faster way to spin?

Although he did not speak, Jenny Hargreaves, his wife, knew he was impatient for the spinning to be done. But she was working as hard as she could. It was not her fault that she couldn't spin as fast as he could weave.

Because she was trying so hard to hurry, the spinning did not go as smoothly as usual, and she began to get nervous and cross. She wished her husband would find something to do besides sitting there with his eyes glued to her spinning wheel.

Suddenly the door opened and their little girl burst into the room.

"Oh, Mother!" she cried. "When will my new dress be ready? It will be made by the day of the festival, won't it? I *must* have a new dress for the festival."

Mrs. Hargreaves' patience snapped. "New dress indeed!" she cried. "As if I haven't enough spinning to do so that your father can fill his weaving orders, without you talking about more spinning for dresses. You sit right down here, Jenny, and card that cotton for me. And don't let me hear any more about a new dress until I have some time to spare."

Poor little Jenny! Her eyes filled with tears. She turned to pick up the cotton for carding. But she could not see through her tears. The child stumbled against the spinning wheel. And over it went onto the floor.

"Oh, Jenny!" cried her mother crossly. "Now see what you have done! It seems that I will never get this spinning finished."

She bent to pick up the overturned wheel, but her husband shouted, "Don't, Jenny, don't! Don't pick it up! I have an idea!"

The two Jennies, mother and daughter, stood side by side, astounded. They looked from the overturned wheel, with its spindle still whirling, to the absorbed expression on the face of James Hargreaves.

"But, James," protested his wife. "You are in a hurry for the yarn. I must get back to spinning. I have so much to do."

"Wait," said her husband, putting his hand on her arm. "I think I see a way to make a spinning wheel that will do your work five times as fast as this one will."

"Five times as fast!" cried Mrs. Hargreaves. "Oh, how wonderful! Then I could do five times as much work as I do now. But how, James? How could you make such a spinning wheel?"

Hargreaves pointed to the spindle, which—although it was now upright—was still turning.

"I can put several spindles side by side," he explained, "and make one wheel turn them all. If I can find a way to draw out the cotton as it is twisted, you can spin five—or even ten—threads at once, and as fast as you can now spin one."

He picked up the spinning wheel and began to examine it, working out his new idea in his mind.

Little Jenny looked up at her mother's excited face. "Mother," she began timidly, "if you can spin five times as fast when Father makes your new spinning wheel——"

Mrs. Hargreaves began to laugh. "Yes, Jenny," she cried, hugging the little girl. "If I can spin that fast, you shall have your new dress in time for the festival."

Hargreaves set to work immediately on his new spinning machine. Although he had to try several different plans before he succeeded, his "spinning jenny," as he called it, was a great improvement over the old spinning wheel. He set up a big frame with a hand-turned wheel at one side. Underneath the frame, in the middle, a row of bobbins held the rovings, ready to be spun. The rovings were drawn up over the top of the frame between two flat boards which could be fastened tightly together, thus holding the rovings firmly. From these two flat boards (called the clove) the rovings went straight to the back of the frame to be fastened to the row of spindles that stood there. When a woman was ready to spin—when the rovings were drawn through the clove and fastened to the spindles—she turned the wheel with one hand to make the spindles whirl. With the other hand she moved the clove forward, stretching the yarn as the spindles twisted it, to make it the proper thickness. Then the finished thread was wound on bobbins underneath the spindles, and she was ready to spin again. As in hand spinning, the machine performed the three necessary operations in order: stretching the rovings, twisting them into thread, and winding the thread on bobbins—only it spun a great many threads at one time.

Thus, to her great delight, Mrs. Hargreaves found that with this wonderful spinning jenny, she could spin TWENTY times as much yarn in a day as with the spinning wheel that little Jenny overturned.

18.

The Cotton Cleaner

How many of the clothes you have on are made of cotton? Your underwear, probably; your dress or your shirt; your socks. Most of our everyday clothes are made of cotton, not only because it wears well and is easy to clean, but because cotton material is very much cheaper than linen or wool or silk.

But long ago cotton cloth was not cheap at all, and there was not very much of it made. Factories could not get enough raw cotton to make into cloth because farmers would not raise it. Farmers would not raise it because they could not make money out of it. They could not make money out of cotton because the fiber stuck so close to the seeds that it was very difficult to separate them. After the crop was grown and harvested, it was long tedious work to pick the cotton away from the clinging seeds.

So you see that cotton could not become plentiful and cheap until someone found an easy way to free the cotton fibers from the seeds. Strange to say, it was a young man from Massachusetts, who had never before seen cotton growing, who invented a machine to do it.

One evening in 1792, Mrs. Greene was entertaining a

group of friends in her plantation home near Savannah, Georgia. The guests were all Southern planters, except for Mr. Whitney, who had recently come down from New England. This young stranger listened quietly to the conversation, which was all about farming.

"What are you going to plant this year?" one gentleman asked another.

"Rice, of course," was the answer. "Rice on all the fields that are suitable. But I have a lot of land that is good for nothing but cotton."

"Will you plant cotton this year?" asked Mrs. Greene.

"What's the use?" replied the planter. "We can't get enough money for our cotton to pay for the work of getting the seeds out of it. The fiber clings so closely to the seeds that it takes one person a whole day to clean just one pound of cotton."

"That is true," agreed Mr. Miller. "It isn't worth while planting cotton. There is no profit in it."

"I wonder," said Mr. Allen, "I wonder why someone doesn't invent something to separate the cotton fiber from the seeds. Why, with a machine to do that, we could all grow cotton and make money!"

"Yes," cried another. "Cotton-raising would be a profitable business, if only we could find someone who could make a cotton cleaner."

Mrs. Greene smiled.

"Well, gentlemen," she said, "if you want anything made, just tell my friend Mr. Whitney about it. He can make ANYTHING!"

THE COTTON CLEANER

The Southern planters all looked at the young man from the North. Whitney was embarrassed.

"Why, I know nothing of cotton raising," he objected. "I have never even seen cotton growing. We do not grow cotton in New England, you know."

"But, Mr. Whitney," urged Mrs. Greene. "You are very clever at making things. Remember that embroidery frame you made for me. And the toys you have made for my children. All the things you have mended on the plantation in the short time you have been here. And didn't you tell me you used to make nails and tools and bonnet pins—even fiddles—before you came to Georgia?"

Mr. Whitney nodded. "That is all true," he admitted. "I have always liked to make things. I studied to be a lawyer, but I think I would make a better inventor than lawyer. However, I could not make the cotton machine these gentlemen want without knowing something about cotton."

No more was said that evening about a machine to separate cotton seed from the fiber. But Whitney did not forget it. In fact, he could not get the idea out of his mind.

The next day he went to Savannah. He visited cotton fields; he saw cotton growing; he got some cotton in the seed; and he discovered how difficult it was to pull that stubborn seed away from the soft fiber.

Mrs. Greene and Mr. Miller (who was the manager of her plantation) were talking together when Whitney returned.

Mrs. Greene noticed the cotton in his hand. "So, Mr. Whitney," she laughed. "You are interested in cotton.

Perhaps you will yet make that cotton seeder we were talking about yesterday."

Whitney nodded seriously. "Yes," he said, looking at the cotton bolls in his hand. "I am going to try. I can see how hard it is to pull the seeds out of this lint. It is a job for steel fingers instead of human hands. I am going to try to make a cotton seeder, but first I must find a place to use for a workshop."

Mr. Miller spoke up quickly. "I can fix a workshop for you. There is a room here where you can work without interruption, and do anything you wish."

Mrs. Greene agreed, and in a short time the shop was ready.

Whitney had already planned the type of machine he intended to try: a revolving cylinder with steel teeth which would reach into a hopper filled with cotton bolls, pull off the fiber, and drop it into a box. But he was handicapped in carrying out his idea by the total lack of materials and tools. He had to make nearly everything he worked with. Even the wire he used for teeth on the cylinder had to be stretched to make it finer. It was slow, discouraging work.

But at last one day he called Mrs. Greene and Mr. Miller.

"I want you to watch my cotton cleaner," said Whitney. "I have made one that will work, I think."

Eagerly Mrs. Greene and Mr. Miller hurried into the little workshop. With deep interest they inspected the crude machine he showed them. They saw a wooden box with an iron grating in it. Underneath the grating was a

THE COTTON CLEANER

wooden cylinder, which was armed with rows of wire teeth. The curved teeth protruded through the slits of the grating, into the top of the box.

"Watch, now," said Whitney. He dropped a big handful of raw cotton into the top of the box. Then he began to turn the crank that was attached to the wooden cylinder. The cotton bolls caught on the wire teeth; as the cylinder turned, the fiber was pulled down through the iron grating. But the seeds were too big to pass through the slits. The iron bars held them back, as the strong teeth pulled the cotton fiber loose. Then the seeds dropped into a box, and the seeded cotton passed on through the grating to drop into another box.

"Splendid!" cried Mrs. Greene. "It works! How proud you must be, Mr. Whitney."

But the inventor looked far from proud. He was frowning as he continued to turn the crank.

Bending over the machine to look at it more closely, Mrs. Greene soon saw the reason for his frown. Most of the cotton fiber, when freed from its seeds, dropped off the cylinder's teeth into the box, as it was intended to. But all of it did not drop off. With each revolution of the cylinder, a little more cotton clung to the wires, until soon the teeth were completely clogged. They would no longer catch the unseeded cotton bolls.

Whitney's hand dropped from the crank. The machine would not work until the wires were cleaned. Something must be done about it. If one had to stop every few minutes to clean the fibers off the teeth, his cotton cleaner was of little use.

Mrs. Greene saw the disappointment and perplexity on her friend's face.

"That's easily fixed," she said with a laugh. "Just brush off the cotton like this." She picked up a hearth brush from the fireplace in the room and swept the lint from the teeth.

"The very thing!" cried Whitney. "A brush! I'll add a revolving brush. I can see how to do it: I'll insert stiff little brushes in another wooden cylinder and place it in back of this toothed roller. If the two cylinders turn in opposite directions, the brushes will remove the lint from the wire at each revolution. The teeth can never become clogged."

The inventor lost no time in thus remedying the defect in his cotton cleaner, and with Mr. Miller's money to back him, he began to manufacture the machines.

Although Whitney and Miller never made any money out of the cotton gin, it was immediately popular in the South. And with good reason: with this little machine, which was turned by hand like a grindstone and no harder to operate, one man could clean as much cotton in a day as fifty men could by hand. In a very short time every planter in the South was raising as much cotton as he could, for with Eli Whitney's cotton gin to clean out the seeds, cotton-raising was a very profitable business. And cotton cloth soon became as plentiful and cheap as it is today.

19.

"*Copy-Cat*"

You have seen wooden toy boats in the ten-cent store. Hundreds of them, all exactly alike. They are cleverly carved, yet they cost only a dime. Did you ever wonder how men could carve those little boats for just a few cents apiece?

The answer is, as you may have guessed, that men did not carve them: a machine did it. A machine so clever that when it is set with a model of the toy to be made, it can turn out hundreds of copies of it in the time it would take a man to carve one by hand. This machine, called a copying lathe, can be used in making so many different things that it revolutionized the manufacture of furniture and toys.

Two men stood in a factory one day in 1818, watching a machine. One man was the owner of the factory. The other was Thomas Blanchard, an inventor.

The machine was turning a gun barrel. Blanchard had improved this lathe so that it finished the gun barrel ready to be put into a stock, or handle. Before that, the machine had only half-completed the barrel, leaving a great deal of work to be done by hand.

Blanchard stood watching the results of his work. Yes, the lathe operated perfectly. He was well satisfied with it.

The factory owner was satisfied, too. This improved machine would cut down the cost of manufacturing guns. He would not need so many men working on gun barrels.

Suddenly, Thomas Blanchard looked up from the machine he was studying. He had heard something that interested him. At a workbench near by some men were talking.

"I guess I'm out of a job," said one. "My job used to be finishing gun barrels. But that improved lathe of Blanchard's does that work now."

"Well," said another as he worked at turning a gunstock. "Blanchard can't take *my* job away from *me*. Gunstocks can't be cut on a machine. He can't make a lathe that will cut gunstocks."

Blanchard smiled as he listened. "So I can't make a machine that will turn gunstocks, can't I?" he said to himself. "Well, I'm not so sure about that. I'll think it over."

As he left the factory, his mind was busy with the idea of a self-acting lathe. A machine that could turn an irregular-shaped object such as a gunstock without the guidance of hands. How could it be made?

For days he puzzled over it. And at last he got the answer from his imagination!

He was driving home one day in his buggy, whistling monotonously to himself as he always did when he was thinking. He was trying to figure out a self-acting lathe. But he was no nearer the solution than when he had first thought of making one.

All of a sudden, a picture flashed into his imaginative mind. A picture of a lathe on which was fastened a real model of a gunstock, and a big block of wood. There were twin wheels on a rod: one wheel on the model and one on the block of wood. The first wheel rolled over the model to feel the shape of it; at the same time the other wheel (which had knives on it) rolled over the block and cut the shape of the model!

Blanchard could see the machine plainly in his imagination.

"I've got it!" he shouted at the top of his voice. He whipped up his horses and raced down the street.

People on the sidewalk stared after him.

"That man's crazy," said one man to another. "He shouldn't be driving."

But Thomas Blanchard was only hurrying home to begin building his lathe. For he saw at last how it should work. It should be a *copying* lathe, such as he had seen in his imagination. The model to be reproduced and a larger wooden block would be placed on a slowly revolving axle. Outside these would be two wheels of the same diameter, one a *feeling* wheel, and the other a *cutting* wheel with sharp cutters around its rim.

As the first wheel, pressed by a weight against the revolving model, felt its way over the contours to be copied, the second, moving in exactly the same path on the block, would remove enough wood to leave behind a precise copy of the model. When once the model and a block of wood were in place, and the machine set, neither hands nor eyes would be necessary to make an exact duplicate of the model. Not only gunstocks could be copied, but furniture, toys—*anything!* His lathe would be a faithful "copy-cat."

And that is just what it turned out to be.

20.

From Father to Son

IN BIG WHEAT FIELDS today the grain is harvested by machinery. In one day a single reaper will cut and bind the grain from thirty acres.

But many years ago, harvesting was long, back-breaking work. When wheat was cut by hand, with a sickle or a cradle, it was the very hardest of farm work. The strongest man could cut only about two and a half acres of wheat in a day, while another man followed to tie the bundles. So you can see how much farmers owe to the invention of the reaper.

In the blacksmith shop on a Virginia farm, Cyrus McCormick stood watching his father one day in 1831. For fifteen years, when he could spare the time from farm work, Mr. McCormick had been working on an invention. He was trying to make a reaper that would lighten the heaviest of farm work: harvesting.

Again and again he had tried the machine, but it did not work well. Again and again he had remodeled it. Now he was determined that this would be his last attempt. Tomorrow he would try out the reaper once more. And if it did not work this time, he intended to give up the project.

126 THE STORY BEHIND GREAT INVENTIONS

Cyrus stood watching his father getting the reaper ready for its test. How he hoped it would work! He knew how much it meant to his father. He had watched him work on it for many years. And he knew, too, how much it would mean to farmers all over the country to have a successful reaper to help with their harvesting.

The next morning the whole family of eight children went to the field of early wheat to watch the trial of their father's reaper.

The clumsy machine was pushed from the back by a pair of horses. Mr. McCormick guided it up to the edge of the standing wheat. Cyrus held his breath as the machine began the task of cutting the grain.

A reel pressed the grain against the cutters, which were circular saws that turned against the edge of stationary knives. The cut grain was pushed onto a platform. When there was enough cut to make a sheaf, Mr. McCormick—walking beside the reaper—would rake it off and bind it.

At first the reaper worked fairly well, for the grain was standing straight and even. But in a few minutes it reached wheat that was bent and tangled. At once the machine stopped. The cutters were choked with grain, and would not turn. The reaper would no longer cut. Mr. McCormick had failed again.

"I'll not fool with this reaper any longer," cried Mr. McCormick. "Take it back to the barn, boys. I am through with it. It is impossible to make a practical reaper."

But Cyrus stepped up to his father.

"Oh, no, Father," he cried. "It isn't impossible. This reaper is good. It can be made practical. I'm sure of it, and

I am going to do it. May I have this machine to work on, Father?"

"Take it," replied Mr. McCormick. "Do anything you want to with it. I hope you succeed better than I have."

So Cyrus McCormick took up where his father left off. He soon found the weak spots in his father's invention, and set to work to remedy them. He made eight important improvements. (1) He placed the horses in front of the reaper, at one side, so that they pulled the machine instead of pushing it. Thus they walked in the stubble along side the standing grain that was to be cut. (2) He put teeth on the wheels, to prevent skidding. (3) He replaced the whirling saws with a moving knife which had saw-like teeth, and moved back and forth to cut with a shearing motion. The knife was moved by a connecting rod and crank driven by the truck wheels. (4) He added wire fingers to hold the grain in place while it was being cut, so that it could not slip side-wise out of the path of the knife. (5) Then he fastened a divider to the end of the reaper's blade—a curved arm which separated the grain to be cut from that to be left standing. Finally he added (6) a revolving reel that would lift any grain that had fallen, and (7) a platform to catch the grain as it was cut. (8) One big driving wheel carried the weight of the machine and also, as it turned, provided the power to operate the sickle and the reel.

By the time another year had passed, the son had proved that a practical reaper could be made. But his work had only begun. Seven more years passed before he sold his first reaper. However, Cyrus never lost faith in his machine. He worked hard advertising his reaper, trying to show farmers how much faster and cheaper they could harvest their grain if they used his machine. And he worked constantly to improve it.

Although several other men invented reapers, McCormick's came to be the most practical and dependable, and consequently the most widely used. And eventually Cyrus McCormick built a great and profitable business out of his reaper. Eventually he proved to farmers all over the country that machinery could do the heaviest of all farm work as well as hands could do it—and very, very much faster.

21.

Mechanical Seamstress

HAVE YOU EVER watched your mother stitch the seams of a dress on the sewing machine? How easy it looked! The dress material traveled swiftly and smoothly under the fast-moving needle. And when your mother stopped the machine and clipped the threads, the seams were stitched firmly and evenly. Good, strong seams in just a few minutes.

But years ago it was different. To make a dress in those days a woman had to sew with a needle and thread, making every stitch by hand. It was a slow process to stitch the seams of a dress. In fact, sewing was such hard work and took so much of a busy mother's time that a young father set to work to find an easier and quicker way of doing it.

In 1843 Elias Howe came home from work one evening very tired, as usual. He was not strong, and his job in Mr. Davis' repair shop was hard work, with very small pay. Every night Elias came home tired and discouraged.

"Come, my dear," said his wife. "Dinner is ready. Let's eat quickly, for I have a great deal of sewing to do after the children are in bed."

"I am too tired to eat," said Elias.

"Oh, come," urged his wife. "You will feel better when you have eaten—although there is not much to eat. Our money is almost gone. Nine dollars a week does not go far when there are so many mouths to feed."

"Money!" said Elias wearily. "If only we had lots of money! Then you and I would not have to work so hard, and the children would have enough to eat and to wear. How I wish I could make more money!"

When the simple meal was cleared away and the children in bed, Mrs. Howe settled down to sew by lamplight. Although she had plenty of sewing to do for herself and the children, she tried to do a little extra for others in order to add to their small income.

Elias slumped wearily in his chair, watching his wife's busy fingers. The needle went in and out, in small neat stitches. In and out, in and out, the needle carried the thread, making a fine, straight seam. The skillful fingers never stopped. On and on they worked.

Elias Howe sighed. He hated to see his wife work so hard. But they needed every penny she could earn. If only there was some way that he could make more money! He would never make much with his work in the repair shop. He must find some other way.

His thoughts went back to an incident that had happened in Mr. Davis' shop many months before. An inventor had come in with a knitting machine he was working on. The machine would not work as he had planned, and he wanted some help.

But Mr. Davis, instead of trying to offer suggestions, had said, "Why bother with a knitting machine? Why not invent a sewing machine instead? Then you would make a fortune."

The inventor had said, "It can't be done. A machine can never take the place of fingers in handling a needle. There will never be a mechanical seamstress."

But Howe had wondered, "Why not?" And he had often wished, in the months that followed, that he could invent a sewing machine that would lighten his wife's work and make a fortune for them.

This evening, as he sat watching Mrs. Howe's busy fingers, he began to consider how a machine could be made to push a needle in and out like that, through cloth. If the needle were sharp at both ends, with an eye in the middle, couldn't it be made to go up and down as the material was pulled along under it?

He was still thinking about this idea when he went to bed, and the next day he set to work to try it out.

He worked for many long months on a sewing machine that tried to imitate the movements of a seamstress' fingers. But the stitches it made were always uneven. And the seams pulled out too soon. The machine was a failure.

Again one evening Elias Howe sat, tired and discouraged, watching his wife sew. It was of no use to work any longer on his invention. He was certain by now that the machine would never really sew. That man in the repair shop—the man who was working on a knitting machine—had been right.

"No machine can sew like a woman's fingers," Elias said bitterly. "I might as well quit."

His wife looked up from her sewing. "Maybe no machine

can sew like a woman's fingers," she said. "But why does it have to? Why not build a machine that makes a different sort of stitch?"

Elias sat up straight. That was a new idea, and a good one. Perhaps he could find another kind of stitch—entirely different from the running stitch that a seamstress' needle made—that a machine could make successfully.

Elias Howe turned his eyes away from his wife's sewing. No need of watching that any longer. He had been on the wrong track in trying to copy her work with his machine. He would start anew. And this time he would succeed.

His weariness forgotten, he began to think of other kinds of needles and stitches.

"Knitting, weaving, lace-making," he said thoughtfully.

"Lace-making!" cried his wife. "Lace-makers use a needle that has an eye in the point. Only the point of the needle goes through the material. Perhaps that kind of needle would work in your machine. It could be fastened securely in the machine and would be much easier to control than the double-pointed needle you have been using, which has to be left free."

"But with an eye-pointed needle, whose point alone goes through the material," Elias said, "a second thread would be necessary. Now, how could I work that? ... Perhaps a shuttle like a weaver uses."

He reached across the table and took up one of his wife's needles. In a few minutes he had snapped the point of it off and had sharpened the head. And there was a needle with an eye at its point.

MECHANICAL SEAMSTRESS

Excited now, he snatched up a couple of scraps of cloth and an ordinary threaded needle.

Mrs. Howe's sewing lay forgotten in her lap as she watched her husband. Would this eye-pointed needle plan really work?

Laying the two scraps of cloth together, Elias pushed the threaded eye of his newly made needle through the cloth and carefully raised it again. A little loop of thread remained beneath the cloth. With his other hand, he thrust his second needle through the tiny loop. Then he drew both threads tight. Again the eye-pointed needle went down through the material and back up. Again the second needle carried its thread through the small loop. Over and over the eye-pointed needle made its trip down and up through the cloth, each time leaving a loop. Again and again the second thread was passed through the loop, and the two threads pulled taut.

At last Elias laid down the two needles. He was ready to test his queer stitches.

Mrs. Howe watched her husband's face as he took a scrap of the cloth in each hand and got ready to pull. How excited and anxious he was! Then his face was shining with happiness, and he was laughing and shouting.

"It works! Look! It works! The stitches hold. I can't pull the pieces apart. Yes, I am on the right track. Two threads—a needle and a shuttle. Now I can make a sewing machine. I can see just how it will be."

Elias Howe sat down at the table and described to his wife the kind of machine he was going to make. So clear was the picture in his mind that, although he worked for many months to complete it, the finished model was exactly as he pictured it that night:

"I shall have a needle with an eye at its point, like this one, on the outside of the machine. The thread will be fed through the needle continuously from a large spool. The cloth will be hung upright on pins that will carry it along, and the needle will go back and forth sidewise through the cloth. On the other side of the material will be a shuttle wound with a second thread. A large wheel at the side, which turns by hand, will thrust the needle through the cloth and pass the shuttle through the loop that the needle's thread makes. That is how I shall make my sewing machine. It will work. I *know* it will work. And this new locked stitch will be stronger than any other method of sewing that has yet been used. I shall make a fortune, and we shall be rich, my dear!"

Elias Howe was right. His machine sewed successfully, and the seams it made were strong and secure.

But it was many, many years before he made his fortune. Years of poverty, hard work and discouragement. Long years of trying to get people to see the value of his invention and to buy his machine. Bitter years of struggle for recognition as its inventor when the sewing machine was finally accepted and widely used.

At last, however, Howe did make a fortune out of his sewing machine, as he had dreamed. Better yet, he lived to see work made easier for busy mothers the world over by his mechanical seamstress.

ELECTRICITY

Magicians of flame—the electric welders

22.

The "Impossible" Motor

ELECTRIC POWER is the basis of modern mass production. Industries of all kinds use it. Everywhere that electricity is available, the electric motor operates mills, factories, farm equipment, home appliances. It is as universal as civilization.

But when the electric motor was first introduced—and for many years afterward—it was not widely used. The early motor was not very powerful, for one thing, nor very adaptable to different uses. Then, too, it was hard to take care of, for the commutator and brushes were apt to get out of order, and repair was difficult. The electrical experts said those troublesome brushes and commutator were necessary, and that a motor could not be built without them. But a young college student did not believe it, and eventually he proved they were wrong.

About 1875, a professor at the Polytechnic Institute of Gratz, in Austria-Hungary, was demonstrating to his class the action of a Gramme dynamo. The machine had a wire-wound armature with a commutator attached to the end. Around the armature was a horse-shoe form of field magnet.

The class watched, fascinated. It was their first experience with an electric generator. One student especially—young Nikola Tesla—was completely absorbed in the performance.

As the armature revolved, the copper brushes, through which the current reached the coil, sparked badly.

"Those brushes shouldn't spark like that," said Tesla to himself, as the motor stopped.

Again the professor started the machine, and again the brushes sparked.

Nikola Tesla was suddenly excited. An idea had just occurred to him. Without stopping to think, he spoke loudly, above the sound of the dynamo.

"A motor shouldn't need brushes and a commutator," he exclaimed. "I think it could be made to run without them."

The professor shut off the motor and looked scornfully at the bold young student.

"A motor without a commutator! Ridiculous!" he said. "That's as impossible as a perpetual motion machine."

One or two of the students snickered, and Tesla flushed.

"Perhaps," went on the instructor sarcastically, "perhaps you are smarter than the electrical experts who design these dynamos. Maybe you can do what they can't—make an electric motor that doesn't need commutator and brushes."

The class laughed, and Tesla, dreadfully embarrassed, said nothing more.

But he did not forget it. Instead, he spent much of his spare time, in the years that followed, visualizing electric

THE "IMPOSSIBLE" MOTOR 141

motors, trying to imagine one without the troublesome brushes and commutator. But even in his imagination he could not make one that would work. The professor might be right after all—but Tesla still did not believe it. There *was* a solution, and some day he would think of it.

Four busy years passed, in which Tesla learned everything he could about electricity. But his "impossible" motor was as far away from reality as ever.

Then one day in 1881, while he was in Budapest studying the telephone system being installed there, he was walking through the park with a friend. He was not consciously thinking of his motor, but was reciting poetry as he walked.

Suddenly he stopped, dumfounded, for he could see in his mind, as clearly as if the real thing were before him, the motor he would build.

"My motor!" he cried. "I see it now! No commutator—no brushes. Yet it will work. I'm sure of it. Look!"

While his friend watched in amazement, Tesla snatched a stick from the ground and began to draw diagrams in the sand.

"See, here it is," he cried as he drew. "This is the armature in the center. It is made of iron bars instead of a coil of wire, and has plates at the ends to short-circuit it. Thus is does not need a commutator or brushes. A rotating magnetic field is set up—a sort of magnetic cyclone. Current is induced in the armature, and the reaction between the revolving field and the induced currents makes the rotable part whirl. Do you understand?"

His friend nodded. "Yes, I understand perfectly. I believe you have a great plan there, Nikola—one that will revolutionize electric power."

And so it proved. Tesla's induction motor, later made just as he drew it there in the sand of the park, has the simplicity, the adaptability, and the power necessary in electric motors for industrial use. It is safe to say that our universal use of electricity for power dates from Tesla's invention of the induction motor—the motor the experts said was impossible.

23.

The Interrupted Lecture

HAVE YOU EVER STOOD on the dock as an ocean liner slipped away from the pier? How big it seemed, towering above you! And when you thought of the part of the ship that was submerged, you realized that the hull of an ocean vessel is really huge. Yet that entire hull was probably one continuous sheet of steel.

Not so many years ago, the seams of a boat's hull had to be riveted together. But with the invention of electric welding, the job of making a better, smoother steel-sheathing was made easier and cheaper at the same time.

Electric welding is important not only in big jobs, such as ships' hulls, airplane framework, or chassis, and building construction; it is equally valuable in very fine work, such as wire manufacturing.

Yet strangely enough, the resistance method of electric welding—which is so important in industry—was discovered by accident.

Young Professor Elihu Thomson was giving his last lecture of the season before the Franklin Institute in Philadelphia. He was demonstrating that all forms of electricity listed in the textbooks are essentially the same in nature.

For a while the experiment went along smoothly, with the audience watching and listening intently. But suddenly there was a hitch. After a discharge of high tension from a series of Leyden jars, the ends of the primary wires, which carried the current, touched each other. When Professor Thomson tried to separate them, he found that they were stuck.

Going on with his lecture, which was nearing a close, he tried to pull the wires apart.

"Thus we have proved," he said, tugging at the wires, "that all forms of electricity——"

Then Elihu Thomson forgot what he was saying, forgot the audience in front of him, forgot that he was in the midst of a lecture. For he had noticed something odd about the ends of those stubborn wires: they were not merely sticking—*they were welded together!* Welded! And by electricity!

At once he saw how he could make apparatus that would weld metals electrically: using low-voltage, high-amperage electricity, he would connect the metal to be welded to one terminal of an electric generator, and connect a rod of metal to another terminal. When the two were brought together, an electric arc would form, melting not only the metal of the plates, but also the welding rod. The two molten metals would flow together and produce a welded joint, which could be perfected by applying pressure.

The professor stared, transfixed, at the wires he held in his hand. Then with a sharp, vigorous tug he separated them at last.

Looking up, he remembered his audience, now impatient and stirring restlessly, wondering at his long silence. With a smile Professor Thomson went on with his lecture, certain that he himself had learned far more that night than any of his listeners.

And he was undoubtedly right. The secret of electric welding that Elihu Thomson discovered in the midst of that lecture has been of tremendous importance in many phases of industry ever since.

24.

The Eye That Never Sleeps

DID YOU EVER SEE a magic door that opens without a touch as you approach it? Or a bewitched drinking fountain whose water begins to bubble as soon as you bend over it? Of course the door and the fountain are worked, not by magic, but by an electric eye—a photoelectric cell. As you approach the door, and as you bend over the fountain, your body throws a shadow on the tiny eye, and it starts a motor which opens a door or turns on the water.

This wonderful little device performs thousands of different tasks—some of them very difficult and particular. It is the basis of television, of wirephoto, and of the perfectly synchronized sound track in talking movies. It counts the cars passing a certain intersection. It turns on street lights when the sun goes down. It prevents accidents in factories by stopping the machinery when a hand or an arm is in the way. It sorts objects by size, shape or color, whatever is desired. It operates burglar alarms. The list of its uses could go on and on, but that is enough to indicate how helpful the electric eye has become. And its possibilities are increasing all the time.

The photoelectric cell was not invented all at once. Many different men have had a hand in its development, to bring it to its present stage of usefulness. It was not until 1924 that the photoelectric cell was first used commercially, yet the principle of photoelectricity was discovered nearly forty years before.

Young Heinrich Hertz was a physicist—a scientist who was interested solely in discovering the truth about matter, not in making practical applications of his discoveries.

In 1887 he was busy experimenting with wireless waves, which he was the first to discover. In the course of these experiments he set up in his laboratory one day two induction coils, one large and one small. Both were connected with a battery. He placed this apparatus in such a way that the spark gaps of the two coils were in line and parallel. Then he began his work.

He varied the larger spark, making it strong, then weak, and measured the effect of these variations on the length of spark in the small gap between the zinc wires of the little coil.

But the feeble sparks were hard to see at the little spark gap. So Hertz built a small box about his measuring device.

And then he noticed something odd. Although he could see them better, boxed in as they now were, the sparks were much shorter.

"Now, why," wondered Hertz, "why would that be? Something is causing this consistent decrease in the length of these sparks. What can it be?"

He considered his apparatus carefully. The change couldn't be due to electromagnetic effect, because the box was a non-conductor of electricity. And yet in some way the box must be responsible for the change.

Hertz removed one side of the box. But still the spark length was short. He replaced that side and removed another. No change. He replaced the second side and removed the third. Still no change.

And then he removed the side of the box which faced the large coil with its wider spark gap. Again he sent current through his apparatus and watched the sparks leap the narrow gap in his measuring device. And the sparks were definitely longer!

"Strange," thought Hertz. "When the other spark gap is in sight, these sparks are longer. When the larger one is screened from sight, these sparks become shorter. There must be some kind of radiation from the large spark that causes the difference."

Hertz experimented tirelessly, and soon became convinced that it was ultra-violet light from the large spark falling on the zinc wire of the small coil which caused the increase in electrical energy, and the absence of such light caused a decrease. In some way, he concluded, the light knocked a little stream of energy out of the zinc and sent it across the small spark gap.

Further experimentation established the fact that some materials were affected much more strongly by light than others, and the light could come from other sources besides a spark.

It was impossible for Hertz, or anyone else of his day, to understand what really happened when light fell on

THE EYE THAT NEVER SLEEPS

his zinc wire. At that time electrons were unheard of. The atom was the smallest known particle of matter. Until it was understood—years later—that each atom is really a little solar system of a nucleus with electrons like planets around it, the photoelectric effect could not be comprehended.

In all kinds of atoms there appears to be a compact center of electrical particles, which is positively charged, and a surrounding scattered group of negative electrons. In light-sensitive substances, such as Hertz' zinc, a wandering electron from the outer edge of each atom seems to be broken away from its orbit by light, thus releasing negative electrons from the substance. These electrons, being negative, are attracted by the positive conductor and stream across to it. In Hertz' experiment, they leaped across the gap and set up the stream of energy he noticed.

The modern photoelectric cell uses this principle. It is a glass vacuum tube, coated on part of its inside wall with a light-sensitive material like potassium or selenium. There are two lead-in wires, one connected to this metallic coating, and the other to a ring of some metal such as nickel or platinum, which is not sensitive to light. When light falls on the sensitive coating, negative electrons are emitted. They are attracted to the metal ring which is kept positively charged. Thus, there is produced instantly, by the action of light, a stream of electrons, that is: a current of electricity. This current stops at once when the light is taken away, and it varies in strength according to the intensity of the light falling on the sensitive plate.

By means of the audion tube this current is amplified as much as is necessary to operate the switches for starting motors, stopping machinery, etc.

When Hertz had satisfied his curiosity about the strange behavior of his spark gap, he went back to his experiments with wireless waves, leaving to others the development of the marvel of our modern age, the adaptable and versatile electric eye.

25.

The Key That Became a Clue

DID YOU EVER BREAK one of your bones? Probably the first thing the doctor did was to insist on an X-ray picture of the break so that he could tell exactly how it should be set. When a baby swallows a safety pin or a button, X-rays are taken to determine the position of the object. X-rays are of the greatest value in medicine and surgery. Their marvelous power of penetrating flesh gives the doctor a window, so to speak, through which he can look into the body before he begins his work.

It is not only in the field of surgery that X-rays are used. In almost every branch of industry these wonderful rays have found a place. They detect flaws in vital airplane parts before they are used, thus saving lives that might be lost if engines were to fail in the air. They show dentists which teeth require attention and which are sound. They bring to light imperfections in pottery that are not visible to the eye. They detect pearls in oysters. They distinguish counterfeit money from genuine.

The list of tasks that can be performed by X-rays is almost endless. Yet fifty years ago they were unheard of.

In the fall of 1895 Professor Wilhelm von Roentgen, teacher of physics at Wurzburg, Germany, was spending most of his spare time experimenting with cathode rays. Hertz had discovered the strange power of these rays to produce brilliant phosphorescent effect in glass and, stranger still, to penetrate thin films of aluminum, wood, and other substances. Roentgen was fascinated by these properties of cathode rays, and experimented endlessly with them. He noticed that any variation in the method of making the vacuum tube, in which cathode rays were produced, varied their performance. In a low vacuum tube, the entire bulb was phosphorescent. In a higher vacuum, the tube was dark but the glass walls glowed. It was a fascinating field for experimentation.

One day, as usual, he blew his own glass tube for his experiments—he was an expert glass blower. This time he made a tube with a large bulb in the middle and bent at either end to form a letter S. He used his own lungs as an air pump to produce the vacuum in the tube, and made as high a vacuum as he could. When the electrodes were fastened at each end, the tube was ready to use.

Professor Roentgen regarded his completed tube thoughtfully. "If I am right," he said, "in believing that cathode rays are streams of electrified particles, and that friction will be developed as they stream past the bends of my tube, then I may see some new phenomena due to that friction."

He darkened his office and then turned on the electric current, which was supplied by an ordinary induction coil. Immediately he saw in the glass walls the same yellow-

THE KEY THAT BECAME A CLUE 153

green fluorescence which seemed characteristic of cathode rays. He covered the tube with a black paper screen, and the glow was extinguished. That yellow light could not penetrate heavy paper.

Suddenly a voice cut through his absorption. "Wilhelm!" cried his wife through the closed door. "Come and eat your lunch. I believe you would never eat if I did not remind you. You would keep on with your experiments until you starved. Come quickly, now, Professor. Quickly."

With a rueful smile, Professor Roentgen laid the vacuum tube on his untidy desk and hurried to obey his wife's summons. She was right. He would never remember to eat if she did not call him.

When he returned to his office after lunch, he exclaimed in self-reproach.

"How forgetful I am! I forgot to turn off the electric current. That vacuum tube has been glowing all the time I have been eating."

He picked up the tube from the book it had laid upon, and proceeded with his experiments, forgetting everything else in his interest in the extraordinary properties of cathode rays.

But again he was interrupted.

"Have you forgotten you were going to take some pictures?" his wife's voice asked from the other side of the door. "It is a beautiful day for photography. Come now, Professor, your experiments can wait."

Again Professor Roentgen laid down the tube, but this time he turned off the electricity. He was an enthusiastic amateur photographer, and he really did want to take those pictures. The experiments could wait, as his wife suggested.

"Now, where is that plate-holder?" he wondered. "I fixed those photographic plates in a holder this morning, so that everything would be ready for my picture-taking. But where did I put it?"

The absent-minded professor looked all over his untidy office. At last he found the missing plate-holder in the clutter on his desk, under the big book he was reading at odd moments. And he was off on his photography excursion.

Late that evening Professor Roentgen developed the pictures he had taken during the day. Most of the scenes were very good. But one puzzled him. In the middle of it was a shadow picture of a large key!

"That is strange," muttered the professor. "I made no photographs of keys. How very extraordinary! Where could this picture have come from?"

He showed it to some of his students who were working in his laboratory. But they were as puzzled as he. None of them could suggest how the silhouette of the key could have got on that plate.

"It looks like your office key, Professor!" laughed one of the boys.

"So it does," agreed Professor Roentgen. "Now where is my office key?"

He went into the office and began to look around. But no key could he find.

At last he called to his wife, "Where is my office key? Have you seen it?"

THE KEY THAT BECAME A CLUE 155

"No," she answered. "Look in your books, Professor. You have probably used it as a book-mark, as you usually do."

Roentgen picked up the large book that lay on his desk and shook it. And out fell the key!

The professor sat down with the key in one hand and the picture in the other, and began to think. The key was in the book. The book was on the plate-holder. And the glowing cathode-ray tube lay on the book while he was at lunch! Could some rays—not the glowing yellow fluorescent, he knew, but some unknown invisible rays—have penetrated both the book and the rubber plate-holder and imprinted the image of the key on the slide?

He would soon find out. He replaced everything on his desk just as it had been at lunch time: Plate-holder, book and key. Then he laid the shining vacuum tube on top of the book, and left it there the length of time it had taken him to eat his lunch.

When the photographic plate was developed, there again was the image of the key. He was right. There were invisible rays (either light, or acting like light) coming from that tube—rays which were able to penetrate glass and solid materials. It could not be the cathode rays themselves, because they were confined within the walls of the tube. What could the mysterious rays be?

Professor Roentgen experimented with these new rays with increasing enthusiasm, and became more and more interested in the possibilities they suggested. Very soon he made a photograph of the bones of his own hand, and thus indicated one of the most important applications of his discovery.

Wilhelm von Roentgen was convinced that he had found a new form of radiation. It was composed of certain invisible rays which were set free when a high pressure electric current was discharged through a vacuum tube, after platinum wire was inserted in either end of the tube for connection with two poles of a battery. When the discharge was sent through the tube, from the anode (or positive pole) bands of varying-colored light proceeded. From the cathode (or negative pole) shot the brilliant cathode rays. It seemed that these cathode rays, where they struck the glass wall of the tube, produced the new invisible rays which he had discovered.

But he did not know what they were. He did not believe they were light. He did not believe they were electricity. They were something new, hitherto unknown. So he called them X-rays.

And X-rays they are called to this day.

26.

When the Furnace Door Snapped

THERMOSTATIC CONTROL of heat is something we are using constantly, but seldom think about. We turn on our furnace on winter mornings and then forget about it, confident that the little thermostat will keep the house at the temperature we wish—neither too hot nor too cold. Your mother puts a roast into the oven and goes about her work, knowing that the heat control will see to it that the meat cooks exactly right. Your water heater keeps a supply of hot water for bathing and dishes and washing, never letting it get dangerously hot—again by the action of that little thermostat. And your mother irons the most delicate materials safely with her automatic iron, which has a tiny thermostat inside it.

Yes, thermostatic control of heat saves us a lot of worry and a great deal of fire hazard. But it was a long time coming into use because no one could design a thermostat small and simple enough to be practical. At last, however, a young Yankee mechanic succeeded where the electricians had failed.

John Alby Spencer was night watchman in a Maine sawmill when he got the basic idea for his thermostat.

His main job was to keep the fire going in the engine room. At first he found this irksome. Pine slabs and edgings were used in the furnace, and while they made a hot fire, they burned down very fast. So Spencer did not dare go very far from the furnace for fear he would forget to tend it in time, and would allow the fire to get too low.

One evening he noticed that the furnace door, a round, iron cover on top of the firebox, occasionally gave a loud snap. As he tended the furnace that night he observed that the snap always came when the fire first burned very hot, and again—oddly, so it seemed—when the fire began to die down.

"That's funny," thought young Spencer. "I wonder what makes it do that."

Hot though the engine room was, he stayed close to the furnace after he fired it the next time to see if he could solve the riddle of the snapping furnace door.

Soon Spencer was laughing. For the solution was very simple, after all. The round iron cover of the furnace heated more quickly at the center than at the rim. When it became hot the metal expanded; and since the expansion was greater at the hot center than at the cooler rim, the tension caused the cover to bulge in the middle. That was what made the *first* snap.

The opposite happened as the fire died down. The center bulge cooled off, and the tension lessened. Then the cover would snap back to its original shape.

"Well, of all things," exclaimed Spencer. "An auto-

WHEN THE FURNACE DOOR SNAPPED 159

matic signal for me! When the door snaps the second time, the fire needs attention. I won't have to stay so close to this hot engine room, now that I know I can depend on the furnace itself to tell me when to build up the fire."

And sure enough, he found that snap of the furnace door, which was loud enough to be heard outside the engine room, was a most dependable warning that the fire was dying down.

Though at first this queer signal amused Spencer, soon he began to think seriously about it.

"Surely that principle of expansion of metals when hot ought to be of some practical value," he thought. "Some day I should find a way of using it."

And years later, he did.

He was working for an electrical company in Boston at the time. Naturally he heard much talk of the thing every electrical company in the country was trying to do: perfect a device for automatically controlling the heat of certain electrical appliances.

One day it occurred to Spencer that there was the practical use for the principle he had learned from the sawmill's furnace door: that a piece of metal, under certain conditions, would change its shape and position.

"Why couldn't I," he wondered, "use a metal disk to turn electrical current on and off? A little piece of metal that would bend when it is hot and thus disconnect the electricity."

It sounded easy, but he soon found it was very difficult to do. For nearly ten years Spencer worked on his thermostat before he perfected it.

Yet when it was finished in 1925, it was just as simple as he had first visualized it: two tiny disks of very thin metal an inch and a half in diameter. They were separated by a little space and fastened together at the center with a small metal post—the whole thing only a quarter of an inch thick. The two metal disks have different heat expansions, that is; one will expand at a lower heat, while the other requires a higher heat. As they lay together at the point of electrical contact, the current flowed through them and they were heated. When a certain heat was reached, one piece of metal buckled, just as the old furnace door used to, and the contact was broken. Thus the heat was shut off before the apparatus could get too hot. When the metal cooled sufficiently, it snapped back to its original shape, and the current was resumed.

So it was that, after many years, the old furnace-door signal taught Spencer how to make our modern thermostat.

CHEMISTRY

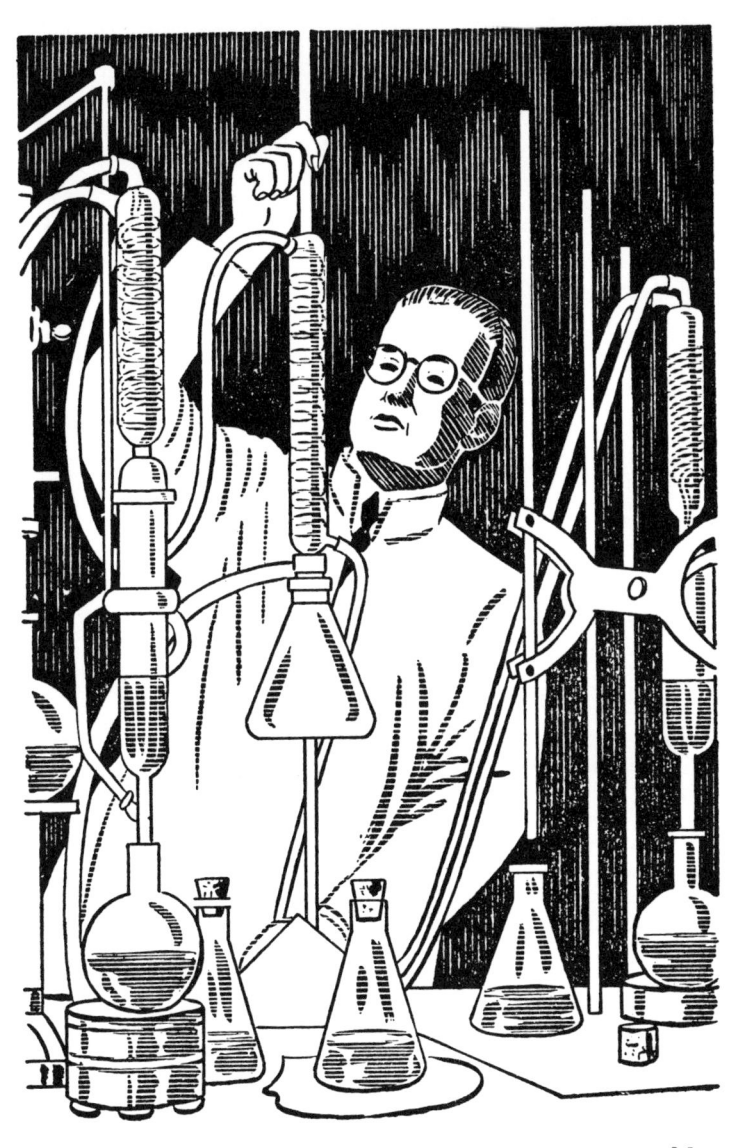

Where myriad secrets of chemistry are still untold

27.

Elastic Metal

Do you realize how often you travel on rubber? Perhaps you wear rubber heels on your shoes. When it rains you undoubtedly wear rubbers or rubber boots. When the weather is nice, you may go for a ride in your father's car: again you are traveling on rubber, for the car could not go far without rubber tires. And the very pavement you ride over may be made of rubber!

We use rubber so often in our daily lives, and in so many ways, that it is very important to us. But a hundred years ago rubber was scarcely used at all, because no one knew how to keep it from melting in warm weather and becoming stiff and hard in cold weather. In those days people preferred getting their feet wet to wearing rubbers, for if the sun should come out the rubbers would stick to their shoes and to the street; and if it should freeze the rubbers would be too stiff to get off. So you see that the man who learned how to make rubber remain firm yet elastic at all temperatures did a wonderful thing for the world.

One evening in 1839 some friends stopped in to see Charles Goodyear. As usual they found him standing over a red-hot stove, stirring something in a big kettle.

"Come in, come in," he cried. "I think I'm on the track of the secret of rubber at last."

"Oh, Charles," laughed a friend. "You have been saying that for years. You have mixed rubber with everything under the sun, and still it is the same old story: either heat or cold ruins it. Aren't you convinced by now that rubber can never be made usable?"

"No, John," answered Charles firmly, stirring the ugly mass in the kettle. "I am not convinced. On the contrary, I am certain there is a way to make the use of rubber practical, and I intend to find it." Carefully he lifted the kettle from the stove and set it on the floor to cool.

"But, Charles," objected another friend. "You can't afford to keep up this experimenting any longer. Think of the money you have spent on rubber and chemicals to mix with it. Think of the time you have wasted that you could have been using to earn money. Think of your family, Charles, and how destitute they are. We came tonight to try to persuade you to go back to your hardware business where you can at least earn a living. We came to try to persuade you to give up this crazy experimenting. You can't afford to go on with it."

Charles Goodyear shook his head stubbornly. "I can't afford to quit," he said. "There *is* a way to make rubber usable. Someone is going to discover it, and I intend to be the one. I shall succeed. I know it. And then I shall be able to take good care of my family and pay all my debts. Don't worry, Tom. I shall pay what I have borrowed from you, just as soon as I find this secret."

ELASTIC METAL

He bent over the kettle and lifted a small amount of the rubber mixture on a spoon. His face changed as he looked at it. His annoyance disappeared, and his boundless enthusiasm for his rubber experiments again took hold of him.

"But look!" he cried. "This is the best method I have ever tried. See! I am mixing sulphur with the rubber gum. It is not quite right yet. Something is still lacking. But the rubber so treated does not get so very stiff with cold, or so very sticky with heat. It is better than any I have yet found."

He took up the cooling bit of rubber from the spoon and held it up.

"See, this is firm and yet it is elastic. I can hold it up over the hot stove, like this, and still it does not become sticky. Of course if it becomes really hot it melts."

"Let me see it," asked John curiously, reaching across the stove.

Goodyear started to put the bit of rubber in his friend's hand, but instead—he dropped it on the stove!

"Well," he cried. "I guess that piece of rubber is ruined now. If there is one thing I have learned for certain, it is that heat ruins rubber. I'll get you another piece." And he dipped the spoon into the kettle again.

While the second spoonful of the rubber mixture was cooling, he took the poker and raked from the red-hot stove top the rubber that he thought was ruined.

Then his friends, watching him, were amazed at what they saw. Charles picked up the bit of rubber and looked at it closely. He fingered it, pulled it, pressed it, with an unbelieving look on his face. Then he began to dance around the room, shouting like a madman!

"Charles!" they cried. "Charles! What is it? Do try to calm yourself." But Goodyear kept on with his wild antics.

"Poor man," thought his friends. "All these years of work and worry have been too much for him. He has lost his mind."

But Charles Goodyear was shouting, "I have it! I have the secret at last! I can make rubber that will not melt! Look! Look! Look!"

Unbelieving, they looked at the piece of rubber he clutched in his hand—the rubber that had fallen on the hot stove.

"See! It didn't melt! Instead, it charred like leather on the edges, and in the center it is perfectly cured. Isn't that the most amazing thing you ever heard of? I just said that if there was one thing certain it was that rubber is ruined by heat. But that isn't true! If the heat is *great* enough, the rubber is cured! By mixing rubber with sulphur and heating it very, very hot, I can make practical rubber. Rubber can now be used for everything—except for food!"

Still doubting, his friends shook their heads. So many times he had thought he had found the secret of rubber-curing. This was just another of his dreams that would melt away with daylight.

But Goodyear did not notice. He had thought of something else. "I must see if cold affects this heat-cured rubber," he cried. "I'll put it out in the snow." And out of the house he dashed, coatless and hatless.

For the rest of that evening, Charles Goodyear was like a madman. Forgetful of his guests, he made experiment after experiment to test his new discovery. And he was happy indeed when he had satisfied himself that he really had found the secret of making rubber usable.

Although he still had ahead of him months of work perfecting the process (discovering the proper degree of heat for a decided hardness), the secret of vulcanization that Goodyear stumbled on that night repaid him for all the years of fruitless experimenting. Rubber treated by his process could be made soft and pliable but without stickiness, or it could be made hard and durable, an elastic metal. So many uses have been found for rubber, since Goodyear's vulcanization process has made it possible to make rubber of every degree of hardness, that his prediction has really come true: Rubber is used for almost everything these days, except food!

28.

The Match That Disappeared

When you buy groceries, they are delivered in paper bags. When you shop in a department store, your purchases are wrapped in heavy paper. When you buy breakable things, they are *packed* in paper—plenty of it. Nowadays, all stores use paper for wrapping and packing, because wrapping paper is so cheap.

But paper was not always inexpensive. At one time it was so dear that stores would not wrap purchases unless it was absolutely necessary—and then they used old newspapers. Really, there was no such thing in those days as the cheap wrapping paper we are familiar with. For all paper was made from cotton, or linen, or rags. And when cotton and linen and rags became scarce, then paper became very expensive. It was not until men learned how to make paper out of wood that our cheap wrapping paper came into use. And that came about through the disappearance of a match!

It was soon after the end of the Civil War.

General Benjamin Tilghman was busy in his workshop with some chemical experiments. He was not working on any particular problem. He was simply experimenting for the love of it.

THE MATCH THAT DISAPPEARED 171

It was good to be home again, after the years of fighting. Good to have peace instead of war. Good to have time to do the things he liked to do. It was good to be home.

The door opened and his brother Richard came in.

The general looked up. "Back from town already?" he asked.

Richard nodded. "Yes, it didn't take me long to take care of my business in town."

"What's the news?" asked the general. "What are people talking about?"

"Oh, reconstruction of the South, of course," answered Richard. "The high cost of living. Food. Clothes.... Cotton is still as expensive as ever—$1.98 a pound. And paper is up another cent—28¢ a pound now. Publishers are saying they will have to go out of business if paper goes any higher. They say they can't put out a newspaper when they have to pay so dearly for paper to print on. Perhaps soon we will have no newspapers to read."

He sat watching his brother work. "What is that, Benjamin?" he asked. "What is in that jar?"

"Oh, just a little sulphurous acid in water," Benjamin answered. "I've been trying a few experiments to see if I have forgotten all my chemistry. I'm through now. But go on," he urged his brother. "Tell me all you heard in town. What are people saying about reconstruction of the South?"

As Richard talked, Benjamin sat idly stirring the acid solution with a long matchstick. He was absorbed in what his brother was saying, and not thinking about what his hands were doing. Finally he broke the match into small bits into the acid. And when the brothers left the laboratory, the broken match was left, forgotten, in the sulphurous acid.

The next morning, when they returned to the workshop, Benjamin started to clean up and put away the materials he had left out the day before.

He picked up the small jar of sulphurous acid and started to empty it. Suddenly he stopped. Something in it had caught his eye. He looked closely at the jar. Then he took a spoon and lifted out of the acid a pulpy, sticky mass.

"What in the world is this?" Benjamin wondered. And then he remembered. "I left a matchstick in this acid. But now it is gone. And what is this pulpy stuff?"

Curiously he examined the soft mass on the spoon. Then he called his brother excitedly.

"Richard! Come here! See what is in this jar."

Richard came across the room to look at the pulpy stuff that his brother was so interested in.

"Why," he said. "That looks like paper pulp. . . . It *is* paper pulp."

"Yes!" cried General Tilghman. "I think you are right. I left a *wooden match* in here. Now it is gone, and I find, not wood, but *paper pulp!* I believe we can MAKE PAPER OUT OF WOOD!"

"Paper out of wood," said Richard. "If only we can! Wood is cheap. If we can make paper from wood, then paper need never again be expensive."

The brothers immediately began to experiment with sulphurous acid and different kinds of wood. And sure enough, after a great deal of careful work, they discovered how to make satisfactory paper out of wood.

THE MATCH THAT DISAPPEARED 173

They chose the whitest parts of wood and cut it into thin slices across the grain. Into a strong lead-lined vessel which was about two-thirds full of water, they put the wood slices. Next they added a solution of sulphurous acid and lime sulphite until the wood was completely covered and the kettle nearly full. They then closed the vessel tightly and turned steam into it until the temperature was raised to 260° F. This heat was maintained for six to eight hours, and then the steam was shut off. The acid solution was drawn off the bottom of the kettle and fresh water forced into the top until the woody fiber was thoroughly washed. At the end of the process the wood was soft enough to be worked into paper by suitable machinery.

It was many years, however, before their process brought down the price of paper. For General Tilghman and his brother ran into a serious problem that was not solved until years later: The acid, which was used to eat into the wood and soften it, also ate into the *container* the wood pulp was cooked in. Consequently, so much money had to be spent buying new containers that the process was very expensive. That meant, of course, that although the wood they used was cheap, the paper made from it was not at all cheap.

But at last someone hit upon the plan of using cement containers. Acid could not eat cement. Thus the process of making paper from wood was perfected, and the manufacture of paper really did become inexpensive. Our cheap wrapping finally became possible, due chiefly to that one little match that disappeared.

29.

The Struggle with Aluminum

Our great modern airliners carry a load of passengers and freight that was thought impossible in the early days of aviation. When airplane bodies were made of wood and steel, the planes themselves were so heavy that the load they could lift was limited indeed.

Today, much of the airplane is made of aluminum, a metal which does not rust or tarnish and is both light enough and strong enough to serve ideally in airplane, railroad and steamship construction, as well as in many other industries.

Long ago, aluminum was recognized as a valuable metal, and the most abundant one on the surface of the earth. But more than a century passed before it was used very much. It is always found in combination with other substances, and is very hard to separate from them. The difficulty of obtaining the pure metal made it very rare and extremely expensive.

Chemist after chemist experimented, trying to find a way of separating aluminum from its ores. Many succeeded; but in every case, the process was so expensive that

THE STRUGGLE WITH ALUMINUM 175

aluminum cost $4.00 or more a pound! What was needed was a cheap, easy method, so that the vast deposits of aluminum could be used in industry. And the man who discovered such a process was neither a chemist nor a mining engineer, but a young college graduate who had studied chemistry just as a necessary part of his classical college course.

One day in 1885, Professor Frank Jewett was telling his Oberlin College chemistry class about the problem of aluminum production.

"Here is a metal," he said, "that is strong, light, rustless—a metal that could be put to thousands of uses. Yet we cannot use it. Not because it is rare. On the contrary, aluminum is the most plentiful of all metals. But we do not yet know how to isolate it cheaply, how to separate it from the earth in which it is found. The chief difficulty seems to be that aluminum oxide has a very high melting point.

"There is a challenge for you young chemistry students—a problem worthy of the best brains in any college. Solve the problem of practical aluminum production and you will be famous. Not only that, you will be rich, for a fortune awaits the man who can do it."

Charles Martin Hall had listened with growing interest. He was a hard-working, clear-thinking student who liked to wrestle with difficult problems. Well, here was a most difficult one—one well worth working on.

Hall nudged Dan Bradley, a classmate, and said, "I'm going after that metal."

Through the remainder of his college days, Hall continued to think about aluminum, though he had no time to concentrate on the subject.

When the school year was over and he was graduated, he asked Professor Jewett for permission to work during the summer in the college laboratory. Delighted that this serious young man was going to tackle the problem that he himself found so challenging, the professor gladly granted his request. And so Hall began to work.

First he hunted out an old text-book of his father's that told all he knew at that time of aluminum.

"The metal may be obtained," the book said, "by heating chloride of aluminum with potassium in a covered porcelain vessel and dissolving the salt out with water. As thus prepared, aluminum is a gray powder similar to platinum, but when rubbed in a mortar it has a distinctly metallic luster. It fuses at a higher temperature than cast iron, and in this state is a conductor of electricity, but a non-conductor when cold."

Hall read this over and over. The phrase "a conductor of electricity" stuck in his mind. When the aluminum ore was heated until it was in a liquid state, it would conduct electricity. Then he would begin his experiments by determining the effect of electricity on aluminum ores.

First of all, he discovered, he must find a cheap, easy method of making the ore fluid so that an electric current would pass through it. He must find something that would dissolve the aluminum earth at a fairly low temperature. It took him months to find such a solvent, but at last, after trying many different substances, he decided, at Professor

THE STRUGGLE WITH ALUMINUM 177

Jewett's suggestion, to try cryolite, a mineral used in the manufacture of soda and glass. He was delighted to find that this mineral liquefied easily at a low temperature, and even more delighted when he dropped in some aluminum earth to see that it dissolved like salt in boiling water.

At once he went to find Professor Jewett.

"I'm ready to try the effect of electricity on aluminum ore," Hall told him. "I've dissolved it in cryolite, and now I'd like to borrow some batteries to try my experiment. Perhaps an electric current will supply a sufficiently high temperature to free aluminum from its ore."

Professor Jewett not only lent him batteries, but went with him to see what would happen when an electric current was sent through the liquid.

To their disappointment, *nothing* happened! The experiment was a failure. Professor Jewett went back to his office in the College, and Hall sat examining his materials and thinking.

Finally his eyes rested on the clay crucible he was using. Maybe that was the trouble. Perhaps he should use another kind of vessel.

It took him only a moment to substitute a carbon-lined crucible for the clay one. Then he placed his electrodes in the liquid and attached them to his batteries. And at once he saw that he had succeeded: some globules of aluminum separated out at one of the poles!

So excited that he could scarcely hold them, Hall picked out the aluminum droplets and ran for Jewett's office.

"I've got it!" he shouted. "It works! Electrolysis does it, Professor!"

"So electrolysis is the answer, after all!" exclaimed the Professor, looking wonderingly at the gray globules. "No chemist thought of electrolysis. And yet it is very simple. The electric current breaks up the chemical compound of the aluminum earth, because the positive pole of the circuit attracts the negatively charged substances, while the negative pole attracts the positively charged elements. Thus pure aluminum collects at the cathode. You have made a great discovery, my boy."

As Jewett had predicted, Hall's aluminum process made him both rich and famous. His simple method, neither slow nor expensive, made rich aluminum deposits quickly available for use. So the price of aluminum went down (in a few years it was less than twenty cents a pound!), and it rapidly became a very popular and widely used metal.

30.

Next to Diamonds

WHEN YOU SEE finished airplanes, locomotives, automobiles, you may think of the many parts that compose them. You may remember the different metals used and the intricate machinery necessary to make all of those parts. But not one person in a thousand ever considers a substance without which airplanes, locomotives, automobiles, and anything else which requires perfectly fitting parts, could not be manufactured: carborundum. Without this electrically made abrasive, which is used to grind metal objects to accurate size and finish, it is safe to say that machine shops, airplane factories, locomotive works, and factories of many sorts would have to close down. Without grinding machinery, industry would be paralyzed.

Carborundum is the world's finest abrasive. It is much more efficient than emery, because it is harder. In fact, it is next to diamonds in hardness, and the diamond is the hardest known substance. Carborundum is used for almost every product of metal manufacturing, from phonograph needles and fountain pens to harvesting machinery and automobiles, because steel and iron can be ground to certain dimensions much more accurately and quickly than they can be cut. Thus industry owes a great deal to the man who discovered how to make carborundum.

One day in 1891, Edward Acheson sat by a small electric furnace in the power house at Monongahela City, Pennsylvania. He was thinking again, as he often did, about a remark made more than ten years before by Dr. George K. King, a famous Tiffany expert of precious stones. Dr. King had said, "The world badly needs a better abrasive than any yet discovered."

For ten years Acheson had dreamed of discovering that better abrasive, and today he intended to begin.

"Diamonds are the hardest things known to man," he thought. "Therefore diamonds would be the best abrasive. But real diamonds are too expensive for wide industrial use. Perhaps I could make artificial diamonds, though. If I could discover how to make artificial ones cheaply, that would undoubtedly be the best possible abrasive."

He went on considering the idea. Diamonds are a form of carbon. Then he would use carbon and see what would happen if intense heat were passed through it.

Acheson searched through his laboratory to find materials for his experiment. He would use powdered coke for the carbon, and an electric current for the heat.

Into an iron bowl he put powdered coke mixed thoroughly with clay. One lead from a dynamo was attached to the bowl. The other lead was fastened to the end of an arc light carbon, which was inserted into the carbon mixture. Now he was ready to start.

He passed a strong electric current through the mixture,

between the lamp carbon and the bowl, until the clay at the center was melted. It was very hot indeed.

Acheson turned off the current and waited impatiently for the stuff to cool. Then he examined it.

"H'm," he said. "Not so good. I don't see any artificial diamonds. Well, I'll just have to try again. After all, I suppose I couldn't expect to succeed the first time. I'll try it a bit differently."

He started to pull the arc carbon out of the mixture. Then he stopped and stared.

At the end of the wire were some bright specks. Curious, he picked off one of the tiny things with a finger. It was an infinitesimal crystal—a beautiful, blue-black, iridescent color.

Acheson picked up his pencil and placed the speck on the end of the lead. Then turning to the window by his bench, he drew the pencil point across the pane of glass.

"Why," cried Acheson delightedly. "This little crystal cut that glass like a diamond! Maybe I did make a form of diamond after all—at least something that is almost as hard."

With a hand that shook from excitement, he pulled his diamond ring off his finger. He would soon find out if he had a substance that approached diamonds in hardness. He would see if it would cut a diamond!

But first he must collect enough of those strange crystals to make a grinding surface. Carefully he gathered the few specks remaining on the arc carbon. Then he repeated his experiment with a mixture of coke and clay until he thought he had enough crystals.

Acheson mounted a small iron disk in a lathe. He oiled the surface and carefully pressed the tiny crystals against it. To his delight, they stuck to the disk. Now he had a grinding surface of his new material.

He set the lathe to turning and held the polished face of his diamond against the revolving disk.

"It works!" cried Acheson after a few minutes. "I can cut this diamond any way I want to. Surely this is a wonderful abrasive I have discovered!"

But he could not rest until he had an expert opinion of his new substance. He worked unceasingly until he had made enough of it to fill a small bottle. Then he hurriedly took the train for New York to see what a diamond cutter would think of it.

On the train he suddenly remembered that he had no name for his abrasive. What should he call it? He thought it was composed of carbon and corundum, and by the time he arrived in New York, he had decided on carborundum for name. (Although he discovered later the substance is really silicon carbide, he kept the name carborundum.)

Acheson took his precious vial of abrasive to an expert diamond cutter and asked him to use it in repolishing the diamond he had experimented on. The cutter was amazed at the efficiency of the new material, and bought the bottle on the spot, at the rate of $800.00 a pound. Carborundum had begun its great career.

Although he still had much work ahead of him, learning to make carborundum in quantities inexpensively, and proving to manufacturers what it could do for them, those little blue-black specks on the arc carbon in his iron bowl proved to Edward Acheson that he had accomplished his ten-year-old ambition: he had made the finest abrasive the world has ever known.

31.

The Substance That Would Not Dissolve

THE USE OF PLASTICS is increasing by leaps and bounds. They are used for knife handles, buttons, phonograph records, billiard balls, combs and brushes, radio cabinets, umbrella handles, fountain pens, steering wheels, electrical outlets and insulation—and that is just the beginning of the list! Nowadays there is much experimental work in the use of plastics in airplane construction, and it may well be that the planes of the future will be largely made of one of these light, tough, almost indestructible substances.

The best known of the plastics—and the oldest—is bakelite. The strangest thing about the history of this valuable compound is that when it was first discovered it was thrown away as worthless, because it was so hard that nothing could be done with it. Eventually, however, it was rediscovered by a man who saw its possibilities.

Leo Baekeland—although still a young man—had retired from business in 1905. He had sold an invention of his, a photographic paper known as "Velox," for enough to live on for the rest of his life. From now on he intended

THE SUBSTANCE THAT WOULD NOT DISSOLVE 185

to do just what he wanted to do—and what he wanted to do was chemical research.

He had long been interested in the idea of producing a substitute for camphor, which had grown so expensive that manufacturers, who needed camphor in their businesses, could not afford to use it.

For many weeks he experimented in the laboratory of his Yonkers home with various combinations, but none of them showed any possibilities of leading to a substitute for camphor.

Then one day he decided to investigate the reaction of formaldehyde on carbolic acid. At once he began to make some interesting and mysterious discoveries, and soon the idea of synthetic camphor was almost forgotten in a new line of research.

The first thing he found out about formaldehyde and carbolic acid was that he got entirely different results when he combined different proportions (adding a little hydrochloric acid to produce a reaction). The results varied when he combined them under different conditions—with more heat or less heat, stirring or not stirring the mixture. Sometimes the solution boiled gently until it became a resinous material which could be used as a cheap grade of shellac. Sometimes a salt-like material was formed that was often used in medicine.

But the biggest surprise came when he tried the experiment on a large scale and used more heat than usual. The mixture started to boil, as it did at other times, but instead of gradually ceasing to bubble, it became more and more violent in its action.

"Look!" cried Baekeland's assistant, Nathaniel Thurlow. "It's like a volcano, spitting out hot particles all over. Be careful you don't get burned."

"Yes," agreed Baekeland, moving back out of reach of the steaming spray, "it certainly looks like a volcano during an eruption."

The men watched, fascinated.

At last the mixture foamed to the top of the glass beaker and overflowed. Then gradually it stopped bubbling and began to cool.

Curiously Baekeland examined the beaker. He found an intensely hard, irregular-shaped, gray-colored mass.

"It looks for all the world like solidified lava," said Thurlow wonderingly. "Maybe you really did make an artificial volcano!"

For the rest of the day the two men worked with that queer hard mass, trying to soften it. But all their efforts were fruitless.

Then Baekeland began a systematic search for a method to shape the substance. Day after day he gave Thurlow a list of chemicals to try on it, while he himself experimented again and again with his formaldehyde and carbolic acid mixture, trying to find a way to control the formation of the stubborn material. But neither of them had any success.

"It's impossible stuff," cried Thurlow at last. "It won't melt, it won't dissolve, it won't soften, it won't break. Even electricity has no effect on it."

"But that's exactly the reason it's going to be a valuable substance," Baekeland pointed out, "when I find out how

THE SUBSTANCE THAT WOULD NOT DISSOLVE

to shape it. Think of the uses for a material that is not affected by heat, acids, or electricity. Why, it can be used in a thousand ways."

Baekeland had already discovered that another chemist had created this same lava-like material some years before. He had thrown it away because it would not melt or dissolve and consequently was useless. But Baekeland would not admit that it was worthless. He kept on trying in every way he could think of, with every known solvent, to soften his new substance. Even after months of unsuccessful experimentation with it, he still clung to the idea of making use in some way of this extremely hard, tough material.

At last he determined that the substance could not be melted or dissolved *after it hardened,* and he concentrated on trying to *mold* it while it was still hot and soft. One day he tried even greater heat than usual, using pressure at the same time. And this proved to be the solution. With a hot hydraulic press he found that he could mold his new material in any desired shape.

Thus, in discovering a way of shaping "bakelite," as he named it, Leo Baekeland laid the foundation for the big industry of plastics, which have become so important in our lives.

32.

Glass That Is Not Glass

DID YOU EVER HEAR of polaroid? If you never have, you soon will, because polaroid—a new kind of glass—promises to be a product of many uses. Worn as sun glasses, it eliminates sunglare. Used in car windshields, it prevents headlight glare. In microscope and telescope lenses, it reveals things the eye can not see with ordinary lenses. A camera equipped with polaroid can take pictures under water. Undoubtedly, this new glass is going to play quite an important part in our lives in future years.

And yet polaroid is not really glass at all!

Edward H. Land found the physics laboratory the most interesting place at Harvard. His physics instructor, George Wheelright 3d, liked to talk—as did Land himself—about polarized light. Both of them knew that what causes the glare in light is the fact that light waves not only move forward in straight lines, but have elements that move at right angles to these straight lines. When light waves are polarized—combed out—there is no glare.

"I made a polarizer for light a few years ago, when I was a youngster," Land told his instructor. "It worked pretty well, although it was far from perfect. I think I could make a better one now. Wish I had a chance to try."

GLASS THAT IS NOT GLASS 189

"I'd like to see you try it," said Wheelright. "The trouble is that it would have to be a cheap, practical, simple method of polarization before it would be of any value commercially. And there isn't really any use working on an invention like that unless you can make it a financial success. There are already several polarizing processes patented, but none is satisfactory for use in industry."

After many such talks with Wheelright, Land decided in 1929 to quit college and work on the problem of polarized light. Wheelright was so much interested in his project that he offered to supply the money Land would need for experimentation and research.

So Land started to work in earnest to devise a method for producing glareless light. For years he worked in secret, with only Wheelright to encourage and advise him. At last in 1932, he succeeded in producing a material that accomplished his purpose. By treating quinine sulphate with iodine, he obtained tiny crystals, which he embedded in a plastic film. He then made a "sandwich" of this film by putting it between two thin sheets of glass. He called his new substance "Polaroid" because it polarizes light waves —gives them a definite direction as they pass through it. Its tiny crystals—a thousand billion of them to the square inch!—lie parallel and in one direction. When ordinary light waves pass through polaroid, they are combed out and untangled. It is as if the waves were passed through narrow slots which make flat parallel ribbons of them. They can only go straight, so there is no glare resulting from waves that cross each other.

When they were satisfied that the new glass could be

produced cheaply enough and in large enough quantities to be of value commercially, Land and Wheelright set up in business, although their laboratory work was still most important to them.

The Eastman Kodak Company was their first customer: they wanted to use polaroid in photographic light filters. With such a big prosperous customer, polaroid was off to a good start. And its business has been growing ever since. During the war, when the necessity for quinine for our armed forces in the tropics cut off the commercial quinine supply, Land began experimenting anew. Eventually he found another substance that he could substitute for quinine sulphate. In fact, he was able to make better polaroid than ever.

PART THREE

INVENTIONS THAT HELP TRANSPORTATION

ON LAND

The ancestor of the modern giant locomotive

33.

The Traveling Engine

PEOPLE LIVING TODAY cannot remember a time when there were no trains. Trains carry passengers from one end of the country to the other in a few days' time. Trains carry heavy freight over steep mountain passes. Trains carry coal away from mines and huge tree trunks away from lumber camps. Trains with refrigerator cars carry fresh vegetables and fruit and meat to people who need them. We cannot imagine a country without trains.

Yet long ago, the idea of pulling cars with a steam locomotive was considered impossible and ridiculous. More than that, people were sure it was frightfully dangerous. Why, the boiler would burst and kill all the passengers! Sparks from the locomotive would set fire to all the houses along the railroad! The smoke would kill birds, animals, grass! Yes, the steam locomotive was undoubtedly too dangerous to be allowed.

But George Stephenson did not agree. He believed that the steam railroad could be a safe, efficient and economical method of travel. And finally he persuaded others that he was right.

In the 1820's a railroad was building in England from

Liverpool to Manchester. It was not intended to be a railroad such as we have now, for steam locomotives were almost unknown. No, this railroad, although it would have cars that ran on tracks, would use horses to pull the cars. At the very steepest hills there would be stationary engines to help pull the load to the top. But steam locomotives—puffing, smoking, dangerous iron horses—no! The idea was absurd.

George Stephenson alone urged the use of locomotives. He had built steam railroads at coal mines with locomotives that could run as fast as fifteen miles an hour on a level track, or pull loads of coal up steep grades at four miles an hour. He was confident that the steam locomotive was the best means of hauling both freight and passengers, and he was very anxious to try it on this longer railroad line, of which he was to be the chief engineer.

But the backers of the new line would not hear of it.

"Steam locomotives would be too expensive," they said. "Look at the coal they burn! They can't pull much faster than horses and they cost much more. Besides, some of those grades on our line are going to be steep. A locomotive could never pull a load up those hills. Only a stationary steam engine can do that, with pulleys."

But Stephenson kept on talking about the advantages of locomotives. He insisted that great improvements could be made, making steam railroading speedy, dependable and safe. Through all the months of work building the road bed and laying the track, he kept on trying to persuade people that locomotives would be far superior to horse-drawn cars.

THE TRAVELING ENGINE

At last the directors of the company agreed to give the steam locomotive a chance.

"We will hold a contest," they said. "Anyone who wishes may demonstrate an engine. If any locomotive can fulfill our conditions we will award it a prize and use it on our line."

So a day was set for the competition, and a prize of two thousand dollars was offered for the best engine that would haul six tons over the new track at twenty miles an hour, or twenty tons at ten miles. The pressure of steam on the boiler must not be greater than fifty pounds to the square inch. There were other conditions, but these were the most important.

Stephenson immediately set to work to build a new locomotive that would satisfy these requirements. As in his earlier engines, he applied power directly to the driving wheels by means of cog-wheels. He also used the forced draft (turning the escaping steam from the boiler into a smokestack), which he had found effective in increasing an engine's speed. This draft made it possible to keep a hotter fire under the boiler and produce more steam.

But to meet the conditions of the contest, he had to have a very large heating surface. So he made a boiler that had twenty-five copper tubes, each three inches in diameter. The tubes, surrounded by water, carried hot gases from the fire-box to the smokestack. Thus he had a greatly increased heating surface, and was able to keep up the steam more easily.

The contest was held at Rainhill, October 7, 1829.

Thousands of people came to see it, not only the directors of the railroad and people in the surrounding country, but people from all over the world who were interested in steam locomotion.

Four locomotives were entered in the competition. There was the *Novelty*, designed by Ericsson; the *Sanspareil* by Hackworth; the *Perseverance* by Burstall; and the *Rocket* made by George Stephenson.

Before the judges arrived, the bellows on the *Novelty* (which were used to create the draft) broke down, and the engine would not work. The boiler of the *Sanspareil* sprang a leak and had to be repaired before it could run. So the judges decided to postpone the contest until the next day.

The crowd was disappointed. They had come, many of them a long way, expecting to see an exciting spectacle. And now there would be nothing to see!

"Well," said Stephenson to his son Robert, "it's too bad these people have come so far for nothing. Let's give some of them a ride."

At once the *Rocket* was attached to a coach containing thirty people, and Stephenson's engine pulled them along at the rate of twenty-five to thirty miles an hour. How amazed and excited those passengers were! They had never traveled anything so fast in their lives.

The next day the contest was held before an even larger crowd of spectators. Eagerly everyone watched each engine's performance.

The *Perseverance* could go only from four to five miles an hour, so it was eliminated from the competition.

THE TRAVELING ENGINE

The *Sanspareil* traveled about fourteen miles an hour, but its pumps got out of order, and it had to stop.

The *Novelty* ran twenty-five miles an hour, but it soon broke down.

George Stephenson's *Rocket* made the specified trip without any trouble, traveling at twenty-nine miles an hour at times, and averaging fifteen. It met every condition of the contest and won the prize.

So Stephenson proved that his faith in the steam locomotive was justified, and he lived to see steam railroads in operation all over England.

34.

Bedrooms on Wheels

HAVE YOU EVER RIDDEN in a Pullman sleeper on one of the new streamlined trains? Remember how smoothly and quietly the train ran, although it was going much faster than a mile a minute? You could walk down the aisle almost as steadily as you can in your own home. You could read or write, or eat soup in the dining car without spilling it—so smooth are the trains of today.

And remember when it was time for bed? You undressed and put on your pajamas just as you do at home. You washed in a nice clean bathroom with plenty of warm water and clean towels. Then you climbed into a soft comfortable bed between snowy sheets, in a tiny bedroom of your own, and went sound sleep. When you woke up it was morning, and you felt fresh and happy, looking forward to another pleasant day on the train.

But years ago it was very different. You wouldn't have liked sleeping on a train in those days any better than George Pullman did. Because of his business as a contractor, that young man had to ride on trains all the time. And he knew just how uncomfortable they were. The engines were noisy, the tracks bumpy, the coaches drafty, and the seats very hard. And as for the beds—but that is the story.

One day in the early 1850's, as the train grumbled to a stop at a station, George Pullman looked out of the window and saw a friend getting on the train.

"Hello, Ed," called George. "Come and sit by me."

The newcomer's heels clattered on the bare wood as he came down the aisle.

"Hello, George. Where are you going?"

The engine started with a jerk. Soon the train was rattling and swaying along at the terrific speed (for those days) of forty miles an hour.

George had to shout to make his friend hear above the noise of the train. "I'm on my way back to Buffalo again."

Ed yelled back, "You are doing plenty of traveling now, aren't you?"

George laughed. "More than plenty! Traveling on trains is no fun. The days are bad enough, with the jolting and the noise. But the nights are worse. The nights are terrible, Ed."

"Why is that?" asked his friend.

"Haven't you ever slept on a train?" Pullman asked in reply.

Ed shook his head. "I don't travel much on trains. Tonight will be my first experience sleeping on one."

"Then," laughed George Pullman, "I won't tell you what it is like. You will soon find out for yourself."

A few hours later, Pullman said, "Ready to go to bed now?"

Ed yawned. "Yes, I'm certainly tired. I ought to sleep fine."

The young men rose from the uncomfortable bench. Holding onto the seats to keep from falling as the train lurched along, they made their way to the sleeper car.

"Look, Ed," said George. "There is your bed. How do you like it?"

Ed looked around, and his dreams of a good night's sleep faded. A row of wooden bunks, with no springs—just thin hard mattresses—stretched along the side of the coach. There were no sheets, no blankets, no pillows.

Ed looked at George Pullman's grinning face. "I'm beginning to see," he observed, "why you said the nights are terrible. How on earth do we keep warm?"

"Oh," George answered, "we can get blankets from that closet back there—if we can find any fit to sleep under."

Pullman led the way to a small closet at the end of the car. From a pile of dirty, ragged quilts and blankets they selected the cleanest.

"Aren't these blankets ever washed?" grumbled Ed.

"I doubt it," sighed George. "In all the trips I've made on these trains, I have never found clean blankets. And it is only lately that they have supplied bedding at all. Before that, we just kept as warm as we could under our coats and shawls."

Back up the car they went with the musty bedding. Soon the two young men were huddled, fully clothed, in their hard bunks, trying to sleep as the train bumped along through the night.

BEDROOMS ON WHEELS

With the first light of day next morning, Pullman climbed stiffly out of bed to find Ed sitting on the side of his bunk, looking very cross.

"What a night," groaned Ed. "I'm more tired than I was when I went to bed."

"I don't see," grumbled George, "why they call this a *sleeper* car. No one can sleep. Even if you could forget the rattle and bang of the train, the hard bed would keep you awake."

Heavy-eyed and weary, the two young passengers stumbled through the coach to the tin wash basin. Several others were ahead of them, and they had to wait in line.

Ed watched the water diminish as each one washed. "What will we do," he asked his friend, "if there isn't any water left in the pitcher by the time our turn comes?"

"We just won't wash," Pullman answered. "There won't be any chance to get more water until the train stops."

He pointed to the single towel that all who washed had used. "And it looks as if there isn't going to be a clean spot on the towel by the time it gets to us."

"Now I believe what you were telling me yesterday," said Ed. "The days on a train are bad enough, but the nights are worse."

Pullman frowned, and he said determinedly, "I tell you, Ed, some day I'm going to build sleeper cars in which people can really sleep. Real beds with good springs and mattresses; clean sheets and bedding; soft pillows. Each bed shall be curtained off so people can undress and sleep just as they do at home in their own bedrooms. Yes, sir! Some day I shall build real bedrooms on wheels, as sure as my name is George Pullman!"

And years later, as everyone knows who has ridden in a Pullman sleeper, he did just that.

His first sleeping cars were merely old passenger coaches remodeled. Although they were crude, they had upper and lower berths which were provided with mattresses and blankets. The lower berths were transformed into seats in the day-time. The upper berths were suspended from the ceiling by ropes and pulleys.

But Pullman was not satisfied with these made-over sleepers. He wanted his sleeping cars to be as beautiful and as well furnished as the most luxurious bedroom. Railroad men said they would be too expensive, but Pullman argued that they would be worth the money. So he proceeded to build brand-new cars to carry out his ideas. Larger, with plate-glass windows, beautiful upholstery, expensive carpets, and complete lavatories—his new sleepers were so comfortable and so beautiful that everyone wanted to ride in them. People grumbled when these new sleepers were sold out, and they had to ride in the older coaches—at lower rates, of course.

Railroad men soon realized that Pullman had been right when he said that the new cars would be worth the money. They found that people were willing to pay for the comfort of traveling in Pullman's "bedrooms on wheels."

35.

Stop!!

Have you ever been on a train, traveling fast, when suddenly the engineer put on the brakes? You were probably thrown forward in your seat by the jolt as every car in the train came to a halt. Of course you wondered why the train had stopped. Perhaps a bridge was out. Perhaps there was another train ahead. Perhaps there was something on the track. Whatever the reason, you knew the engineer had seen danger ahead and you were thankful he was able to stop the train in time to prevent an accident.

When your grandfather was a boy, train wrecks were much more common than they now are. For although trains did not travel half as fast as they do today, they could not be stopped half as quickly. But finally a young man decided that there must be a way to make a brake work instantly on the entire length of a train, so that an engineer could stop at once when necessary. And he set out to find that way.

As George Westinghouse was coming home from a business trip one day, the train he was riding on came to a grinding stop. He stepped from the train to see what was the trouble. On the track ahead he saw the wrecks of two other trains. His train could not go on until the track was cleared.

George walked up to the scene of the accident, where a crowd had gathered.

"How did it happen?" he asked a man standing near. "Surely the engineers must have been very careless to have crashed into each other on a straight stretch of track like this."

The other man shook his head. "No," he answered. "It wasn't carelessness. It was the brakes. I watched the crash. The engineers saw each other. Both tried to stop. But the brakes wouldn't work in time."

"Were the brakes out of order?" asked Westinghouse.

"No," the other replied. "Not out of order. Just too slow. You see, the engineer has to signal the brakeman, and the brakeman has to put on the brakes. And then the brakes themselves can't stop a fast-moving train very quickly. After all, a train that has many cars can't be stopped in a moment. It's impossible."

"Why is it impossible?" George Westinghouse wondered. "Why can't some sort of brake be invented that will stop every car on the train almost instantly? A brake that can be applied by the engineer, without waiting for a signal to the brakeman? After all, the engineer is the one who sees the danger. He is the one who should be able to stop the train."

As he rode on home that day, Westinghouse kept studying the problem. And he decided to invent a quick and certain brake that would make train travel safe.

But he soon found that *deciding* to do it was one thing,

and *doing* it was quite another! For what power could be used to extend the entire length of a train and brake all the wheels at once? He found that steam wouldn't do. It would not work in cold weather, because it condensed too fast. Chains wouldn't do, for chains long enough to extend the length of a long train were too heavy. Nothing that had ever been used as brakes would do. He must plan an entirely different type of brake. He must find a different kind of power. But what would it be?

One day at noon he sat at his desk in his father's factory. He was writing down all the different kinds of power he could think of, trying to find one that would operate his brake. Steam, gas, water, wind——

The door opened. Someone came into his office.

"I'm busy," said George, without looking up from his paper. "I haven't time to see anyone."

"I'm sorry to bother you," said a young woman timidly. "I just want to see if you will subscribe to this new magazine." She held out a copy of *Littell's Living Age*.

"No," answered Westinghouse. He looked up from his work. "I haven't time to read. I'm trying to work out an invention. An important invention. I have no time for magazines."

The girl turned away. But George had seen how disappointed she looked.

"Wait," he said, laying down his pencil and reaching for his purse. "I'll subscribe for your magazine. Let me see it."

George took the magazine and turned the pages carelessly. Suddenly he stopped. An article had caught his attention: Compressed air was being used as power for digging a tunnel through the Alps.

"Air!" cried George Westinghouse. "Compressed air! There's my answer! That's one power I never thought of to operate my brake. And it is the one thing that will work! Air can be piped for thousands of feet through the mountains, and still have power enough to drive a drill through solid stone. Then air can be carried the length of a railroad train, and still have force enough to set the brakes on every car. An air brake! That's what I'll make."

And he did. On the locomotive he put an air-storage reservoir and a steam-driven air-compressor. In the engine cab he put a three-way valve. A pipe for air ran the length of the train, joined by hose and couplings. On each car was a brake cylinder. By means of the valve, the engineer let air into the pipe and the car cylinders, and the air forced the brakes against the wheels. When the engineer was ready to release the brakes, he let out the air.

The air brake was successful on its very first trial, but Westinghouse saw that improvements were needed. He put a reservoir of air on each car. He also changed the whole plan so that lowering the pressure of the air in the train line (which would happen if any part of the braking system should give way) would cause the brakes to set. Thus any fault in the brakes would stop the train before an accident could occur.

Before long the air brake was adopted for use on all trains. And so today train travel is safe, even with far greater speeds than were used in those days, thanks to the air brake that George Westinghouse invented.

36.

The Engine That Has No Spark Plugs

Though the steam engine, the gasoline motor and the electric motor are all very important in transportation today, there is a fourth type of engine that is being used more widely all the time: the diesel. New streamlined trains carry diesels to drive the generators which furnish electricity for the motors. Submarines use the combination of diesel and electric power. Huge trucks, tractors, ocean vessels—all find the diesel motor a cheap, efficient source of power.

Like most inventions, the diesel has been so improved during the last few years that the inventor—if he were alive—might have difficulty in recognizing a modern diesel motor. Yet the honor of originating the basic idea of this engine will always belong to Rudolph Diesel.

During his college course at the Munich Technical Institute, two things happened to Rudolph Diesel which changed his entire life: he heard something, and he saw something.

What he heard was a lecture by Dr. Carl von Linde, one of his instructors, in which the professor pointed out that the best steam engine of that time wasted 90% of the energy of the coal. Ninety per cent! That statement started Rudolph Diesel thinking about the possibility of making an engine that would use all—or nearly all—of the energy of fuel.

What Diesel saw was a cigar lighter. It had a cylinder in which air, heated by the compression of a plunger, ignited some combustible substance. Compressed air gets very hot. The more you compress it, the hotter it becomes. Maybe, thought Diesel, maybe that principle could be used in making an efficient motor. Maybe—some day...

After being graduated from the Technical Institute of Munich, Rudolph Diesel became an assistant to Professor von Linde, who was working on the development of ice and refrigerating machines.

This work with refrigeration machinery deepened Diesel's already keen interest in thermodynamics: the science of the mechanical action of heat. As he studied heat-producing machines, he became obsessed with the idea of making one that would be different from any yet known—one that would be cheap, simple, safe, and far more efficient than any in use at that time.

He was already familiar with the steam engine, of course, which was only 10% efficient, according to von Linde. The new internal combustion engine, or gasoline motor, was better. But that was expensive to run, was quite complicated (requiring a carburetor and an ignition system), and was really a fire hazard, since gasoline is so explosive.

Diesel thought about heat-producing engines for several

THE ENGINE THAT HAS NO SPARK PLUGS

years. What power could be used that was cheap, safe, and effective? And what method of using it?

At last he thought of oil: an internal combustion engine using a mixture of oil and air, instead of gasoline and air. That, he thought, could be made successfully.

After many experiments, but before he built a single complete engine, Diesel wrote a paper on his idea. He called it, "Theory and Construction of a Rational Heat Motor."

When this paper was published in 1893, it drew a great deal of attention—but most of it was ridicule. A few people, however, understood the importance of Diesel's idea. Among these was Friedrich Krupp, a big steel manufacturer in Germany. At once he sent for Diesel.

"Your engine sounds as if it might be an important new development. It would certainly be cheaper to operate than the motors now in use. Oil is much less expensive than gasoline. But I still do not understand exactly how your motor will work."

Diesel was glad to explain. "It is a four-cycle engine," he said. "On the first, or intake stroke of the piston, air is drawn into the cylinder. On the second, or compression stroke, the air is compressed until the pressure is five hundred to six hundred pounds to the square inch. This compressed air is very hot—about 1000 degrees Farenheit. On the third, or power stroke, the heated air ignites the fuel oil which is sprayed—in a very fine spray—through nozzles into a compression chamber. The oil burns very fast, and the expanding gases that result force the piston downward, delivering power to the shaft by means of a connecting rod. On the fourth, or exhaust stroke, the burnt products—waste gases—are expelled through an exhaust valve. You see, no spark plugs are necessary, and no carburetor. It is a very simple engine."

Krupp considered for a while. Then he nodded thoughtfully. "Yes, I believe it will be worth while to help you develop your engine. We will supply the money you require to build an experimental motor."

So Diesel, having worked out the plan of his engine in great detail, started in to work it out in actual practice.

At first diesels were slow in coming into common use, in spite of their economy. They had to be very large and heavy to withstand the high pressures used. Their great size and weight were serious drawbacks. But in recent years light, strong metals have been developed that take the place of the heavy iron and steel that Diesel used. Thus the diesel became usable in many ways. Modern diesels are so light that they may soon be used in airplanes.

37.

Quantity Cars

Today nearly every family has a car. People do not have to be rich to own an automobile, for there are cheap cars for those who haven't much money, as well as expensive cars for those who have plenty of money.

But when automobiles were first made, *all* cars were expensive. Only a few rich people could afford them. It was not until a young man determined that he could make cars cheaply if he made a lot of one kind that cars became as common as they are today.

In a steam-engine factory in Detroit one day two young men were working together assembling an engine.

"It's no use, Henry," said one of them at last. "This piston rod won't fit that cylinder."

"No," said Henry. "Nothing ever fits anything else in this factory. Nothing is ever made twice alike. It's so wasteful, Bill. And I hate to see waste."

Bill laughed. "Oh, we won't waste this rod. We will just grind it until it will fit the cylinder."

"But that's what I mean by waste," said Henry. "We waste half our time making things fit that should be made to fit in the first place."

"Well, the factory pays us for our time," Bill replied. "Why should you care whether you are paid for putting together well-matched cylinders and piston rods, or for making them fit? You get the same amount of money. It's the factory's waste, Henry, not yours."

"That's just it," Henry answered, as the two young men worked on the over-sized piston rod. "It's the factory's waste that bothers me. Everyone would benefit if they didn't waste so much. It would work like this: If they produced perfectly-fitting parts, we workmen could do twice as much work assembling machines. The expense for wages would then be cut in half. So these engines could sell for less money. If they sold for less, more people would buy. Then the factory could be enlarged and could build twice as many engines. So the owners would make more money, and they could afford to pay us higher wages. Don't you see how much better off everyone would be if there was no waste of time or money?"

Bill laughed again. "You make it sound easy, Henry. Just like the 'House That Jack Built.' Why don't you build a factory of your own and show us how to do it?"

"Some day I'm going to," said Henry Ford seriously. "I'll have a watch factory. Every part will be made by machinery, and made so perfectly that all the workmen will have to do will be to put the parts together. There will be no wasted time, no wasted materials, no wasted energy. Bars of steel will go in at one end of the factory, and finished watches will come out at the other end. The more watches I make, the cheaper I can sell them. I'll be able to make them so cheaply that everybody in the country can afford a watch."

But Henry Ford did not build his watch factory. Before many years had passed, he decided that something else was needed more in this country than a cheap watch: a cheap automobile.

Cars were already being built. But they were very expensive. They were complicated to operate, and extremely difficult to repair. It was almost impossible to find new parts that would fit when old parts gave out.

Ford decided he would build a factory that would make one cheap, simple car. A car that anyone could drive, because it was so easy to operate. A car that anyone could repair, because all parts made in the factory would fit it perfectly. A car that anyone could afford to buy, because he would build so many he could sell them cheaply.

But first he had to design such a car.

It would take too long to tell how he worked night after night making his first car. How he built another, and another, until he had a car that would fit his purpose. How he raised the money to start his factory. And how at last he really accomplished what he had dreamed: In 1912 Henry Ford built a car that was so cheap and easy to run that it had a widespread sale. Thus he made so many that he was able to sell cars even cheaper.

Although automobiles have been improved so much since that they do not look much like the first car his factory made, all car factories in the United States today use Henry Ford's method: The parts are made by machinery so perfectly that all the workmen have to do is to put the car together. An endless belt carries the car from one workman to another. Each puts on one part or performs one operation. There is no waste of time, or energy, or materials. Into one end of a factory go bars of steel and out of the other end come—not watches—but complete automobiles.

38.

At the Touch of a Toe

IN ALL THE BUSINESS of driving a car, nothing is simpler than *starting* it: just turn the ignition key, put your toe on the starter, and the car is ready to go.

But thirty-five years ago, any other part of driving was child's play compared with starting the motor. A driver set the key on the magneto, retarded the spark, then got out of the car prepared to work. He took hold of the crank at the front of the car and pulled out the choke beside it. Then he spun the crank a few times, released the choke, and gave the crank a quick, hard turn. Sometimes the motor kicked over and he rushed back to the wheel to advance the spark before the motor died. More often, nothing happened, and he spun again. And *sometimes* the crank kicked back and broke his arm.

All in all, a man was lucky in those days to get his motor running within twenty minutes, without injuring anything but his temper.

So the man who put car-starting at the touch of a toe did a great thing for the automobile industry—and a greater thing for the automobile driver.

One July day in 1910, Charles F. Kettering sat in the

office of his friend, Mr. Leland, president of the Cadillac Company.

Mr. Leland looked downcast and serious. Another of his workmen—the fifth within a very few weeks—had just broken his arm cranking a car.

"Mr. Leland," said Kettering thoughtfully, "I believe it wouldn't be very hard to crank a motor by electricity."

Leland looked up, interested. "You really think so?"

Kettering nodded. "Something like the starter I put on the cash register—a little electric motor operated by a button."

"Electric starting would be a wonderful thing for the automobile industry," said Leland. "But can it be done? Lots of men have suggested it, but no one has shown a practical way of doing it."

"Well," said Kettering, "I think it is possible. I'm going to try it."

All the way back to Dayton on the train, Kettering thought about the self-starter problem. He knew it had been talked of for years—in fact, there were several patents on file telling how to use a generator, driven by a gas engine, to charge a battery. Driving the car would make the generator charge the battery, and there would be the current for the starter.

But what if you drove a long time without using the starter? Then the battery would become overcharged. How could that be avoided?

By the time he reached the Dayton barn that he called his factory, Kettering was certain that electric starting was possible but he still had no idea how it could be worked.

AT THE TOUCH OF A TOE 219

For weeks he and his small staff experimented with different batteries, motors, and various-sized gears. They kept careful records of every experiment, careful figures of different voltages and amperages that they used. But they could not see that they were getting anywhere.

Then one day Kettering received a letter from the engineer of the Cadillac Company: "Please send one of your self-starters to be installed in a car for testing. We are getting ready to bring out our new model, and equipment to be used on it must be approved in the very near future. If your starter is satisfactory, Mr. Leland intends to install it on all new Cadillacs. How soon can you send one?"

"How soon, indeed," Kettering wondered. He had no self-starter yet—no model at all. All he had were two notebooks full of drawings and figures and experiment records. Two notebooks and—at last—the right idea. For he had finally figured out how to take care of the battery-charging problem: He would use two coils—one that carried a lot of current, which was necessary to crank the engine, and one that carried just enough current to charge the batteries. The coils were to be wired in reverse, so that the first bucked the second. Therefore, no matter how fast one drove, the generator could not overcharge the battery.

The starter itself would be a small gear, on a spring, that would fit outside the flywheel. Pressing a button would push the small gear into place beside the flywheel, and make it turn. There it would revolve the larger wheel. When the motor was turning fast enough, the small gear would slip, on its spring, back to place.

Kettering wrote the Cadillac Company that he would send a starter as soon as he had one to send. Then the barn became a scene of feverish activity. Long hours Kettering and his boys worked, putting gears together and wiring generators to batteries; then taking all apart when the apparatus would not work, and starting all over again with different sizes, different tie-ups.

Weeks went by, and the self-starter seemed no nearer success than ever. To make matters worse, another letter came from the Cadillac Company, urging some definite information. Another man was working on a self-starter of a different type. If Kettering could not complete his in time, they would have to consider the other's.

But Kettering knew he was on the right track, and kept on working. And at last they made a starter that worked —it actually started the old motor they kept in the barn for experimenting.

Now he wanted to test the starter himself in a real car, so Mr. Leland sent a new Cadillac to Dayton by express.

When the car arrived, Kettering and his staff eagerly ran out to see it. They looked it over inside and out. And the longer they looked, the more puzzled and unhappy they became.

"Boss," said Bill Anderson finally, "*where* are we going to *put* our starter?"

Kettering shook his head. "I don't know, Bill. I see where it *ought* to go, but there's no room for it. Those Cadillac engineers didn't leave any space for our starter. We can't put it in after all."

"You mean we can't use our starter after working on it all this time?" cried Bob De Maree.

"I mean," explained Kettering, "that we will have to make it over and make it smaller—much smaller."

Back to the barn they went to start all over again—only this time they knew what they were making. They designed a smaller generator, made the parts, and assembled it. But it wasn't small enough yet. So they began to make another still smaller.

They had just one week left to install a starter in that Cadillac. In one week the car had to go back to the factory, and if it did not have Kettering's self-starter in it they would lose their big chance with Cadillac Company.

No factory staff ever worked harder than Kettering and his men labored during that last week. Day and night, almost without sleep, living largely on coffee to keep awake, they worked—wearily, stubbornly, endlessly.

On the very last day of the week, they finished the new starter. Carefully, they fastened it all in place, battery on the running board, generator and starter gears under the hood, starter button inside the car. Every wire was in place, every bolt tightened.

Kettering climbed into the car and pressed the starter button. And then all of them felt that life was not worth living, for—after all their work—the starter did not go! Nothing happened when the button was pressed—nothing at all!

In desperation they sent for a friend, Bill Cryst, who had helped them all along in his spare time. It did not take him long to locate the trouble in the wiring. Kettering and his men were too tired from their week-long grind to know one wire from another. But Cryst soon straightened out the difficulty, and again Kettering stepped on the starter. This time the weary, anxious men heard a beautiful sound—the throb of a running motor! Kettering's self-starter was a success—a success in time to get the two million order from Cadillac!

Other automobile manufacturers quickly followed Cadillac's lead. Soon the difficult, dangerous crank was entirely replaced by Kettering's starter that worked at the touch of a toe.

39.

No Road Required

You've heard much of the importance of the tank in World War II—that fighting monster that climbs over trenches, barbed wire, shell holes, and knocks everything out of its way as it goes. You know that the tank was the basis of Hitler's blitzkrieg, that it enabled the Allies to land artillery and supplies for the invasion of Europe. In short, you know that the tank is an indispensable machine in modern warfare. But did you know that it is merely a younger brother to a machine which is indispensable in peacetime?

The tank is an outgrowth of the caterpillar tractor. This amazing engine is a jack-of-all-trades. It travels where no other vehicle can go, in mud, in marsh, over logs and undergrowth. It performs all sorts of difficult tasks, from logging in almost inaccessible swamps to clearing snow from city streets. It needs no road, for it lays its own track as it goes.

The caterpillar tractor began life as a farmer, and while it has given way to the lighter wheel-type tractor for most farm work, it is still called in for hauling gang plows and harvesters over the big fields of the West, where it was born.

"Uncle Ben" Holt, as he was familiarly called by all of his friends and associates, stood with his brother Charles in a huge wheat field near Stockton, California, watching one of his Holt Combined Harvesters at work.

When he had come to California from New England, several years before, in the 1880's, Holt had been amazed at the vastness of the ranches, at the large-scale farming that was carried on in the central valleys of California. Why, one of the fields was as big as a county back home! It wasn't surprising that some of the ranchers claimed they set out in the spring to plant a field, and by the time they started back the grain was ripe and could be harvested on their return trip to the ranch house!

Benjamin Holt had been quick to see that California farmers needed more and better machinery. His first step was to combine the harvester and the threshing machine then in use into a single machine that harvested the grain, threshed it, and delivered clean wheat in bags.

His Combined Harvester had been successful from the start, but to Holt it was just a beginning. Power was necessary to pull it. And so he had turned to building traction engines for the purpose.

It was the latest Holt steam tractor that the two brothers stood watching that day near the beginning of the twentieth century—a huge machine with a thirty-six-foot wheel spread! Heavy, clumsy, and awkward, the traction engine was not a great success.

"It won't do," sighed Ben regretfully. "It works fine on smooth, solid ground, but the wheels bog down in this swampy soil. We've got to have something that will work

NO ROAD REQUIRED

in this soft delta land around the head of the San Joaquin River."

"Wider wheels is the only answer," said Charles. "If you get them wide enough, the wheels can't sink."

"No," objected Ben. "We can't make the wheels any wider. I've got a thirty-six-foot wheel spread now—eighteen feet on each side. No. That tractor is too heavy already. Wider wheels would only make it worse."

"What are you going to do then?" asked the older brother. "Give up the idea of tractors and let the ranchers go back to using horses to pull the harvester?"

Absently Ben wiped his already dirty face with a piece of grease-covered waste he took from his pocket. "I don't know how I'm going to do it," he answered slowly, "but I'm going to make a traction engine that works—one that can travel on any kind of soil."

For months "Uncle Ben" Holt struggled with the problem of wheels that wouldn't mire down in the soft delta soil. But the difficulty seemed insurmountable. The wider you made the wheels, the more traction you had; but, at the same time, the heavier the machine became, then still more traction was necessary. No, wheels wouldn't do at all. He had to find something else. But what would it be?

At last Holt came across the idea of the lag-bed, a continuous belt track laid down and picked up by sprocket wheels. Several men had thought of the idea, and some had used it on various machines, from bicycles to wagons. But it remained for Benjamin Holt to develop and improve the principle to the point of commercial success.

Day after day in the "nursery" of the Holt factory

(the part of the shop in which he worked out his inventions) he sweated over his crawler tractor, testing, tearing down, figuring, changing, reassembling—completely absorbed in his work. He never heard when the factory foreman told him they had orders for more of the wide-wheeled traction engines—orders that should be filled immediately. He scarcely knew whether he had his meals or not. Night and day meant nothing to him. All he could think about was his new tractor with the continuous track, and the many problems that still had to be solved.

Just as the rest of the Holt family decided that something would have to be done to make Ben rest, he announced that his crawler was ready to test.

Every factory worker, as well as all the family and numerous neighbors, were on hand in the street in front of the Stockton factory to see how the queer vehicle operated. In place of wheels the tractor crawled on two belts, whose outer surfaces were corrugated to provide a better grip on the soft ground. Inside each belt were two lines of steel rails in short sections, hinged together. Five wheels, within the belt, turned on the rails by means of pulleys and a cogged mechanism, and moved the track forward. Thus the tractor ran on its own self-made track and was not dependent on the condition of the ground or road underneath it for traction. As in his old engines, there was a high seat for the driver, who steered by means of two clutches. Each belt had a clutch, and when the driver wanted to turn the tractor, he disengaged the clutch on the side of the desired direction. That track stopped turning, and the other track crawled on around. When the machine was headed the way he wanted to go, the driver again engaged the clutch and the tractor moved forward.

The watchers cheered as the new machine crawled steadily down the street and over the field. "Uncle Ben" had again made an engine to help the farmer.

But Benjamin Holt frowned as he watched his assistant turn the tractor and begin the return trip to the factory.

"What's the trouble?" he muttered. "That engine is shaking all over. If that keeps up, the thing will shake to pieces before it has a chance to wear out. What in time is the matter with it?"

Back to the "nursery" went the crawler, and back went Ben for more long hours of work. More testing. More figuring. And finally he cured the vibration. Such a small thing had caused it: When all five of the pulleys within each track were the same size, the belt flopped violently, causing the tractor to shake and quiver. But when he made one of the wheels smaller than the others, and consequently the pulleys a different size, the belt ran evenly; the shaking stopped.

Again the tractor was tested. Down the street; over freshly plowed fields; up steep grades. On it went steadily and smoothly. It pulled heavy loads; still no shaking. Holt's tractor was a success.

"I've got it! I've got it!" he yelled when there was no further room for doubt. "This fellow can go anywhere and do anything."

And he was certainly right. Successful as it was with steam power, it was even more practical as soon as he changed to internal combustion motors. Today the caterpillar tractor pulls the heaviest of loads over the roughest of roads, in forests, in jungles, over snow and ice, through swamps. Whenever roads are lacking that wheeled vehicles can travel, men call in the caterpillar, and many of them are "Holts."

IN THE WATER AND IN THE AIR

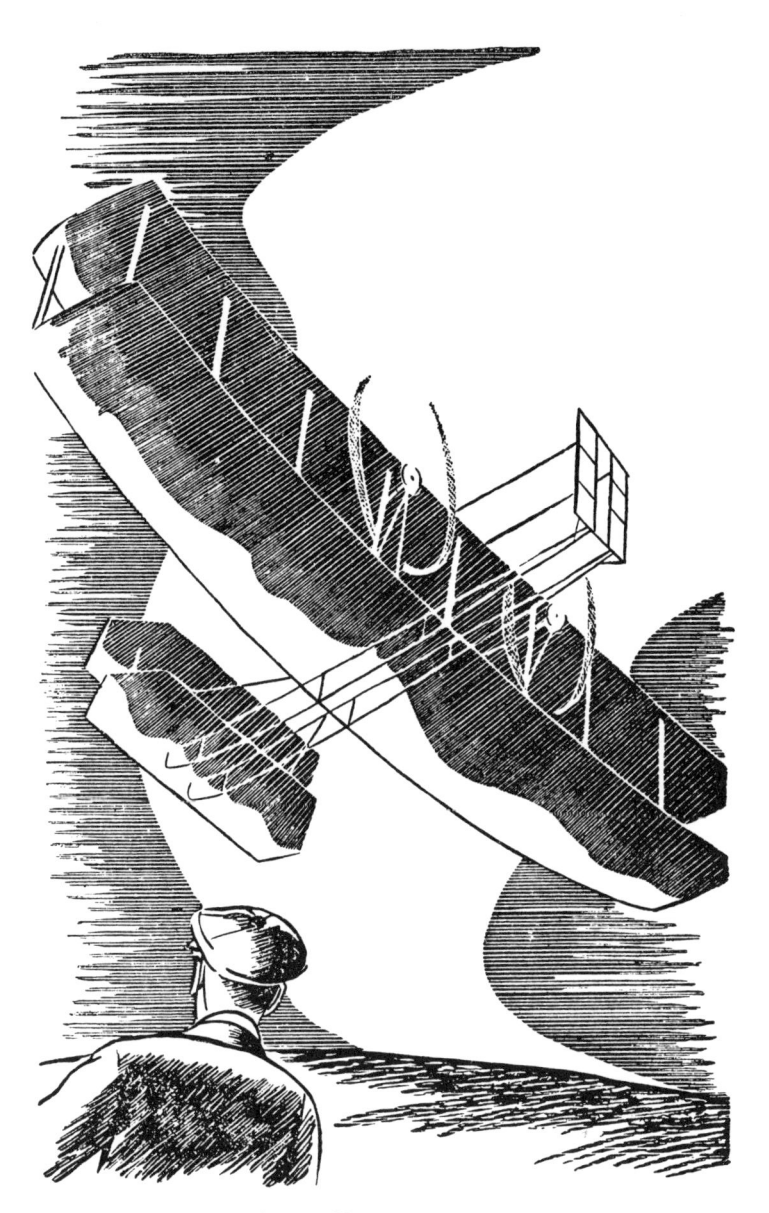

Early challenger of the air

40.

"Fulton's Folly"

TODAY OCEAN LINERS cross the Atlantic in a week, and the Pacific in less than two weeks. Today ocean travel is fast and safe in peace time, and very, very pleasant.

But for two hundred years after the *Mayflower* brought the Pilgrims to America, ocean voyages remained slow and dangerous. Sailing ships were dependent on the wind for their speed. They were at the mercy of the wind in a storm. It was not until men learned how to use James Watt's steam engine in boats that water travel became dependable.

About 1802 two men stood one day on the bank of a canal near Birmingham, England. One was an Englishman, the Earl of Stanhope. The other was an American artist, Robert Fulton, who had come abroad to study art.

"We need canals in my country," said Fulton. "If some of our wide rivers and large lakes were connected by canals, we would have a long waterway reaching from the Atlantic Ocean to the Mississippi River."

"America is such a big country," said Lord Stanhope.

"Yes," agreed Fulton. "Its bigness makes travel difficult. Long journeys on horseback or stagecoach are very hard. With a waterway across the country, we could travel a great deal of the time by boat. How much easier that would be!

"Still," the American went on thoughtfully, "boat travel is not easy, besides being very slow, when one must paddle up-stream. We need power-driven boats to make travel really pleasant."

"Well, why not build a steamboat?" asked the Englishman. "I am going to make one myself some day."

"I've often thought about it," said Fulton. "However, it is easier said than done. Many men have tried it. But no one has made a steamboat that will travel fast enough and smoothly enough to be really practical."

"That is because they haven't built their boats properly," Lord Stanhope said. "They don't use the right kind of propellers."

"I think that is true," agreed his friend. "I think a practical steamboat can be made, if one could just find the best kind of propeller."

"Now my steamboat," went on Lord Stanhope. "My steamboat shall have propellers like a duck's feet. They shall close as they go forward through the water, and then open to push back."

Fulton considered this idea for a few minutes. "No," he objected at last. "I don't think that would work. There would be too much resistance from the water. Your boat wouldn't move fast enough."

All the way home the friends discussed steamboats. Then Fulton said, "I am going to try out different kinds of propellers. I shall make a small boat model, and make

"FULTON'S FOLLY"

experiments with it. In that way, perhaps I'll learn how to build a good steamboat."

At once he set to work on his model. He made a boat four feet long and one foot wide. Two strong clock springs provided the power.

One after another, Fulton tried different kinds of propellers with the little boat. He tried the type Lord Stanhope suggested, which was like a duck's foot, and opened and closed as it went through the water. He tried an endless chain of small square floats, called chaplets. He tried two paddle wheels at the sides of the boat. He tried a paddle wheel at the stern. He tried side oars, and various other kinds of propellers.

At last Fulton decided he was ready to make a big boat, powered with steam. His experiments with the little boat had been very valuable. Not only had they convinced him that side paddle wheels made the best propellers, but he had discovered how large the paddles must be in proportion to the size of the boat. And he had learned how much power was necessary to move a boat of a certain size.

His first big steamboat was not successful. Nor was his second. But Robert Fulton did not give up. Five years after his experiments with a model—in 1807—he built a third boat, which he called the *Clermont*. Everyone laughed at him for trying again what was seemingly impossible. Even the men who lent him money for building this third boat insisted that their names be kept secret. They were afraid that they, too, would be laughed at for spending money on "Fulton's Folly," as the *Clermont* was jokingly called.

The *Clermont* looked very queer to the people of that day—and it would have looked just as queer to you. It was a clumsy, ugly craft, with all of the machinery right out on top of the deck! On each side of the boat a great uncovered paddle wheel projected. The paddles creaked as they turned, and splashed water on anyone unlucky enough to be near. Smoke and sparks flew from the huge smokestacks, and some fell on the passengers. But however queer it looked, the *Clermont* really worked! Up the Hudson River it steamed at a better speed than any boat had ever made before, covering the 150 miles to Albany in thirty-two hours. Everyone was amazed.

So the laugh was on the scoffers after all. The *Clermont* was a success. Immediately after its trial run, it began making regular trips on the Hudson from New York to Albany. Ten years later it made the trip in only eighteen hours. And "Fulton's Folly" turned out to be one of the greatest advances ever made in transportation.

41.

"*The Fenian Ram*"

THE SUBMARINE is an important member of any large navy today. Equally at home on the water and in the water, fast, easily maneuvered, it is a vital part of defense and attack.

Though men have experimented with submarines for at least one hundred fifty years (Robert Fulton built one before he started work on his steamship), it is only in the last thirty years that they have been used very successfully. A large measure of the success of the modern submarine is due to an Irish patriot who worked almost his entire lifetime trying to perfect undersea craft so that it would be a weapon with which to destroy the British Navy.

John P. Holland was a good American, and had been for many years. But he could not forget his native Ireland and his lifelong dream of her freedom from England. He was convinced that the British Navy would have to be destroyed before Ireland could be free, and he had been working for years on designs for an undersea torpedo boat, which he hoped could sink British men-of-war.

Thus when, in 1891, the Fenian Brotherhood, a group of Irish patriots in America, was looking for some means of helping Ireland, Holland suggested his undersea boat.

"Nothing but a submarine boat," he told them, "can possibly block the English Navy. A fair-sized fleet of undersea boats, such as I have planned, could easily keep the English fleet in its home waters. Then Ireland would be able to fight England without being menaced by its navy."

"Perhaps you are right," admitted John Breslin. "But I'm afraid it would cost more than we have. We can't get much money together for our cause, you know."

Holland nodded. He knew that lack of money had always been a big handicap in the Irish fight for independence.

"Well, I'll see what the others say," said Breslin. "I will let you know."

A few weeks later Holland was notified that the Fenian Brotherhood would finance the building of his submarine, and Holland went happily to work.

At the foot of West 13th Street in New York, he built his boat. The first boat was a failure, and he built another. This second boat was the first successful submarine ever made. It was thirty-three feet long, shaped somewhat like a cigar. It carried a crew of three—pilot, engineer and gunner. It was run by a petroleum thirty-horsepower engine. Beneath the floor were ballast tanks and valves. There were no air flasks, but two large air compartments, from which air lines supplied air to the interior of the boat and to the engine.

For its first trial, Holland took it to a breakwater in Jersey City. Many of the Fenian Brotherhood were gathered to watch it. Most of them were dubious when they saw the queer-looking craft. Was it for this they had spent their hard-earned money? What could that long, narrow, iron cigar do to the British Navy?

They watched in glum silence as Holland and his crew climbed into the strange boat and shut the conning tower after them. Then they were amazed to see the bow of the boat dip under the water! Head first, that queer craft was diving into the ocean. In a few seconds not a sign of it remained on the surface.

"Well," said one of the watchers. "Maybe we were too hasty in judging Holland's invention. If he can sink into the water without a trace, like that, he could sneak up on the biggest man-o'-war in Britain's Navy and shoot a torpedo into her side."

"Yes," agreed another. "It looks like John P. Holland has the best sea weapon we have ever seen."

Just then a newspaper reporter came up. "Where is this boat we've been hearing about that can sail under water?" he asked jokingly. "I hear it is going to run the British Navy out of existence."

The Irish patriots closed up like clams. Not a word would they say. They wanted no publicity for their submarine now. That might spoil their plans.

"All right," laughed the reporter at last. "If you won't let me see it, and you won't tell me anything about it, I'll just have to use my imagination in describing the *Fenian Ram*."

And use his imagination the reporter certainly did! He described Holland's boat in such wild, impossible terms that people laughed at the idea of such a vessel. And the name "Fenian Ram" stuck to it thereafter.

Although the Fenian Brotherhood never built a fleet of submarines, as they had hoped to do, to fight the British Navy, the building of those boats gave Holland invaluable training and experience. Thus when, in 1893, the United States Navy advertised for plans for submarines, Holland was ready. He submitted designs which were accepted, and he began the building of submarines for the American Government, which he continued until his death. So the weapon he originally designed for his native Ireland he gave to his adopted country, America.

Although many vital improvements (such as the periscope for seeing above the water when submerged, the combination of diesel and electric motors for safer and more certain power, and the gyrocompass for certain steering) have been added to the submarine since those first boats were built, the name of John P. Holland stands foremost in the history of undersea navigation.

42.

The Third Rudder

HAVE YOU EVER watched an airplane zoom overhead, and wished that you might fly? And you probably said to yourself, "I *will* fly some day, too. I'll fly an airplane when I grow up."

Many years ago men used to watch birds sail overhead, and wish that they, too, might fly. But unlike you, they did not *know* that they would ever be able to do it: they only *hoped* they would. At last, however, soon after the beginning of the twentieth century, two brothers found out how to fly, and they learned by watching the birds.

Wilbur Wright looked up from an article he was reading and watched his brother put the last nail in their new glider.

"Another man crashed in a glider, Orville," said Wilbur.

Orville laid down his hammer. "What was the trouble?"

Wilbur turned back to the magazine. "He hit a fresh wind current, and he could not shift the wings fast enough to ride it properly. His plane turned over and crashed."

Orville nodded thoughtfully. "That's the trouble with

depending on the flyer's body to shift the wings. It isn't fast enough to be safe. So long as the pilot has to shift his own weight to turn the plane, flying just isn't safe. We must find some other way of balancing our plane. We must find some safe and sure way of changing the wings to suit the wind."

"Yes," agreed Wilbur. "Our airplane must be safe. And automatic balance is essential to safety. We have a rudder that steers the plane from side to side. We have a rudder that guides it up and down. Now what we need is a sort of *third* rudder that will control side-to-side seesawing, caused by changing winds. A third rudder to enable the plane to keep its balance."

For weeks the Wright brothers thought about this problem. They knew that air does not blow in straight, regular currents. It is constantly changing, tossing, whirling, falling. An airplane must be able to combat this changing air pressure in order to keep its balance. They knew that until they solved this problem they could never make a safe airplane. And a safe airplane they were determined to make.

One day when the brothers were trying their glider on a hillside they stopped to watch a hawk soar overhead.

"He flies just as our glider should go," said one brother. "His outstretched wings are borne up by the air currents. He guides himself with his tail."

"Yes," cried the other. "And look! He tips his wings a little. Perhaps that is the way he balances against the wind. Perhaps that is the third rudder we are looking for."

The brothers stood watching the bird until it was just

THE THIRD RUDDER 243

a dark speck against the sky. Both were thinking the same thing: "If we can warp one wing a little, maybe we can control side-to-side seesawing. Maybe warping the wings will balance the plane."

They lost no time in trying out this idea for a third rudder. They built a box-like glider frame of spruce and steel wire. The double-deck wings, curved slightly like a gull's, were covered with cloth. The aviator lay flat across the center of the lower wing. Cords ran from the wing tips and were fastened to his body. As in riding a bicycle, the driver bent his body to balance himself, but did not have to shift his position. This movement of his body pulled the cords that raised and lowered the wing tips. In this way, the machine was balanced against the wind, as the air pressure was varied on different parts of the wings, and the driver could keep his machine from turning over.

Crude and clumsy as this machine was, it was the first practical airplane, the father of our modern airliners. For the Wright brothers' balancing scheme, to their joy, really worked. Warping the tip of one wing up, and the other one down, as the driver bent his body, really did balance the glider against changing winds. At last they were on the way to making a practical, safe airplane.

They spent many more months experimenting. One of their most important lines of experimenting was with air currents. They built the very first wind tunnel. It was only an old stovepipe through which they blew air. But in it they were able to study the effects of air currents upon small models of their gliders, hung inside. Thus they were able to tell how different wing-shapes were affected by air-currents, and how strong a wind was necessary to hold up a certain size plane. Wind tunnel experimenting that the Wright brothers started has taken much of the guesswork out of aviation.

Orville and Wilbur built many more gliders before they built a real airplane with an engine. But at last they were successful. In 1903 they built a motor-driven plane that was controlled by the pilot, and was not at the mercy of changing winds. Their "third rudder," which later developed into *ailerons*, made the modern airplane possible.

43.
The Toy That Works

IT TAKES A real storm nowadays to upset the schedule of the airlines. Blind-flying instruments have been made so dependable that fog, clouds, rain or darkness hold no terrors for trained pilots.

A very few years ago, however, airlines had no schedules to speak of, because pilots could not fly safely unless visibility was good. Flights were canceled at the least sign of bad weather, and were thus so irregular, and flying so hazardous, that few people cared to travel by plane. It was not until a toy—a spinning top—which had already been used to make navigation safer on the water and under the water, was applied to air travel, that blind flying became safe and dependable.

Elmer Sperry Jr. had been familiar with the gyroscopic top as far back as he could remember. When his brother and he were small, his father had brought home one of the fascinating toys. It was a simple little thing—merely a small fly-wheel so mounted that it was free to turn in any position around its center of gravity, the only fixed point. Once started spinning in any direction, it would firmly resist all attempts to change that direction.

A simple toy, the gyroscopic top, but it had completely changed the lives of the Sperry family.

Elmer A. Sperry Sr. had seen the possibilities in the balancing properties of that spinning top. He had put the principle to work in the gyrocompass, which gives ocean liners and submarines a dependable guide for steering that is not affected by the iron used in the ship's construction. He had put it to work in the "metal mike," which steers ships automatically. By the time Elmer Jr. had grown to manhood, the word "gyroscope" was inseparably connected with the name "Sperry," and he was as familiar with gyroscopic principles as was his father.

One day in 1928, Jimmie Doolittle, an Army flyer who had already made a name for himself in aviation, came to the office of Elmer Sperry Jr.

"I want some blind-flying instruments," said Doolittle. "Real ones that we can depend on—not like these unreliable things we have to use now."

"What do you want me to do?" asked Sperry.

"Make them."

"But I don't know a thing about aviation," protested the inventor's son. "I never flew a plane in my life—don't know the first thing about it."

"That's all right," answered the Army man. "*I* know aviation. *You* know invention. You have helped your father on his gyroscopic inventions for years, haven't you?"

Sperry nodded.

"Then between the two of us we ought to be able to work out some really good blind-flying instruments."

And Elmer agreed, his mind already busy on the problem.

Months of work followed. Sperry learned that a magnetic compass was even less reliable in an airplane than on a ship; not only was it affected by the steel in the airplane, but the turning, accelerating and vibrating of the airplane made the compass swing badly. Following a magnetic compass in air navigation resulted in a zigzag course, and blind landings were almost impossible.

At first Sperry and Doolittle tried a small edition of a ship's gyrocompass in an airplane. But they had to give it up. The apparatus was much too heavy, and there was too great an error resulting from the airplane's high speed.

At last they worked out two instruments which are the basis of blind flying today. These two important instruments, both based on the gyroscope, are called directional gyro and gyrohorizon.

Accurate steering needs a fixed object for reference, such as the sun, a star, objects on the ground or a compass. The directional gyro provides a fixed direction, which is set by the ordinary magnetic compass at the start of the flight. It has a circular card, which, like the gyro, remains fixed as the airplane moves around it. When flying blind, the pilot keeps this card in line with a spot on the front of the instrument. Then he knows, whether or not he can see where he is going, that he is heading in the right direction.

It is amazingly easy, in an airplane, to lose all sense of horizontal and vertical. A pilot could be flying upside down and think he is right side up. In clear weather he can tell by looking at the horizon whether he is flying level, or whether his ship is climbing or diving. When he cannot see the real horizon, he looks at his gyrohorizon. A pointer bar is connected to the gyro to represent the horizon. A yellow miniature airplane is painted on the dial in front of it. As the plane banks, climbs, or glides, the miniature plane does the same, but the pointer is kept horizontal by the gyroscope. The pilot knows he is flying level when the little airplane silhouette is in line with the horizon bar and parallel to it.

Compact, light and dependable, the two instruments that resulted from the combined efforts of Elmer Sperry Jr. and Jimmie Doolittle—gyrohorizon and directional gyro—took the guesswork out of blind flying. They soon became standard equipment on all airlines, and are the basis of automatic flying today.

44.

Anchored Airplane

THE OUTBREAK OF World War II necessitated immediate expansion of our Air Forces. That meant, of course, speeding up production of aircraft of all types. It meant, too, training a sufficient number of pilots to operate the planes *by the time they were built.* That sounds easy, doesn't it? But pilots are not trained in a few days. There is more to combat flying than merely taking off and landing in broad daylight. Pilots must be well versed in blind flying: depending on instruments, and not on their senses, for safe operation of their planes in all kinds of flying conditions.

When all of this instruction was done in actual airplanes in the air, it was very expensive in money, in time, and in lives. A man's first mistake might be his last, costing his life and wrecking his plane. Now, however, much of the pilot's training is done on the ground, in an *anchored* airplane which reproduces the conditions of flight without its dangers. And what is more, thorough training is accomplished in half the time.

Edwin A. Link Jr., the son of an organ manufacturer of Binghamton, New York, was an instructor at a local airfield in 1927. After a flying lesson one day, he watched his student climb out of the plane. The boy was so excited he tripped over himself.

"I'm doing pretty well, don't you think?" he babbled. "I can really fly now, Mr. Link."

"Sure, Jack," answered Ed Link. "You did fine. You'll make a good pilot—be ready to solo after about eight more hours in the air."

The amateur flyer grinned at his young instructor. "Flying's fun," he announced. "I get a kick out of every minute in that plane."

As the boy walked off, Link muttered to himself, "Yes, he'll enjoy those eight hours of flying, but I'll be bored stiff. Teaching is nothing but drudgery. The same thing over and over. Wish I could figure out some way of teaching kids to fly without taking them off the ground until they know how to handle an airplane."

That was probably an absurd idea. How could anyone learn to handle an airplane without leaving the ground? A plane is like no other vehicle. It moves, not on tracks or roads or buoying water, but on air—unstable, unpredictable air. Obviously, the only way to learn to control a plane in the air is to operate it in the air.

Link shrugged and dismissed the subject from his mind as he went home to dinner.

But the problem of training flyers on the ground wouldn't stay dismissed from his active mind. It kept bobbing up at all times and places, bothering him increasingly. And one day he found the answer, in the building he had known better than any other all his life, except his home: his father's organ factory.

ANCHORED AIRPLANE

Watching—as he had watched countless times before—the workmen installing the bellows system in a cottage organ, Ed Link suddenly saw a way to make a training machine for flyers: A miniature airplane cushioned on air, yet anchored safely to the ground. A bellows system was the answer—compressed air!

All winter long, Link experimented in the organ factory with bellows and wind vents. By spring he was building a model in a corner of the factory. Before the year was over he had made a machine that could be made to behave like a plane in flight.

It consisted of a small fuselage—just big enough for a man to sit in comfortably—with wings and tail unit. The dummy airplane was mounted on a universal joint, which in turn was mounted on a turntable. Thus the machine could turn to left or right, nose up or down to a fifty degree angle, and could also tip diagonally, or "bank" as planes do in turning. Movement was controlled by stick and rudder pedals, attached to valves which controlled vacuum-operated bellows. Vacuum was supplied by an electric turbine in the base of the trainer.

Ed's brother George was the first student to learn to fly in that first Link Trainer, in 1928. After a fast but thorough course in the miniature airplane, George got his solo wings with less than an hour in the air! Ed Link had accomplished what he wanted. With his ingenious machine he could set up at will any flying conditions a pilot would ever expect to meet, and teach him the proper way to handle his plane—without taking him off the ground.

As time went on, Link improved his trainer immeasurably, building into it everything new that came out in aviation. When instruments for blind flying came out, he found that his trainer was a "natural" for teaching their use.

Some of the details of the modern Link Trainer are very complicated, since it is necessary to make things happen artificially that would happen naturally in actual flight. For instance, in real flight, when the speed of the airplane drops below a certain minimum, the plane stalls and sometimes starts to spin. To make a spin result from too-low speed in his trainer, Link uses the same vacuum-line for the stall bellows that supplies the airspeed regulator bellows. So long as normal airspeed is maintained, suction from this vacuum line keeps the stall bellows closed. But when airspeed drops, the suction is reduced and the bellows automatically opens, sending the trainer into a spin. A diagram of the way this apparatus works reminds one of the involved series of operations in a Rube Goldberg cartoon!

But if the construction of Link's trainer is complicated, its operation is simplicity itself—exactly like the operation of a real airplane. The pilot turns, banks, dives, gains altitude, or comes out of a spin by using the same controls in the same way he would in an actual plane. Being cushioned on air and unstabilized, he has all the sensations of flying, except forward motion.

Although his trainer had immediately proved itself efficient years passed before it became a commercial success. Not until the need of instrument training for flyers became felt did the Link Trainer come into its own.

45.

Sun on Earth

How much do you know about the A-bomb and the H-bomb? Everybody knows at least three things:
1. The A-bomb is tremendously powerful.
2. The H-bomb is incredibly *more* powerful.
3. Both bombs utilize atomic energy.

But did you know that the two bombs are based on entirely different methods of releasing atomic energy? The A-bomb's force comes from the *splitting apart* (called "fission") of atoms, while the H-bomb uses energy generated by a *putting together* (called "fusion") of atoms.

Did you know that the H-bomb would be totally impossible without the A-bomb—unless the bomber could make a trip to the interior of the sun? Actually, the A-bomb is a giant fuse for the mammoth firecracker which is the H-bomb.

And did you know that, while the A-bomb was made first, the theory of the H-bomb had been known long before the A-bomb was dreamed of? For many years, scientists had been aware that the sun's energy (heat) comes from the fusion of hydrogen atoms to form helium. If the sun can do it, why couldn't man? Two words answer that question: temperature and pressure. Nowhere on earth was

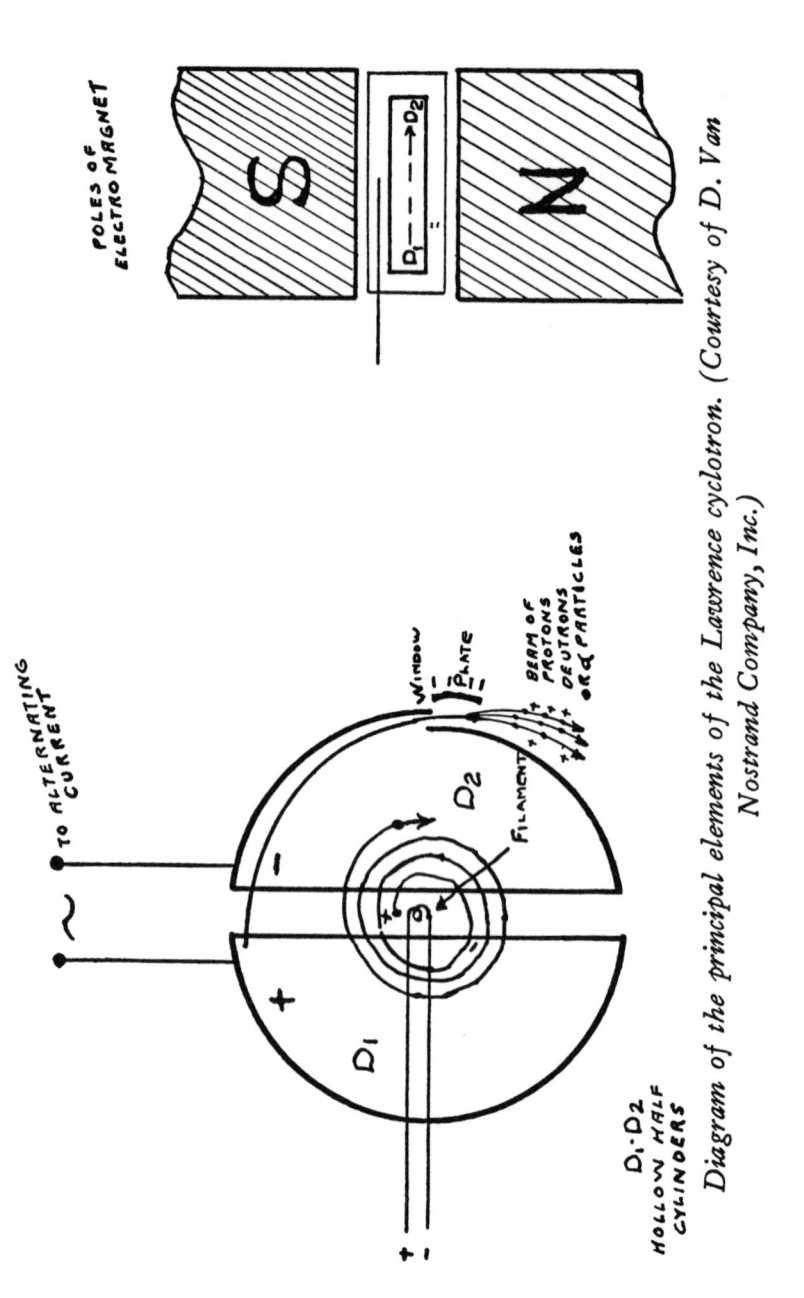

Diagram of the principal elements of the Lawrence cyclotron. (Courtesy of D. Van Nostrand Company, Inc.)

there a fuel which could produce the heat necessary for hydrogen fusion, or a furnace that could hold such heat without melting away; no materials on earth had sufficient tensile strength to hold the necessary pressures. The idea of producing tremendous energy from the fusion of hydrogen atoms remained merely a theory, until the A-bomb was set off over Hiroshima.

A great many discoveries led up to the A-bomb. Three of the most important of these, perhaps, were: (1) that the atom is not indivisible; (2) that there is such a thing as nuclear disintegration, of which radio-activity was the first example; and (3) that mass and energy are the same.

For many, many centuries the atom had been considered indivisible. It was thought to be the very smallest possible particle of matter. Since the largest atom is only about one-hundred-millionth of an inch in diameter (and many are much smaller), it would seem that this view of the atom was reasonable enough. But just before the beginning of the twentieth century, scientists discovered electrons, those infinitely smaller particles of atoms which are negatively charged with electricity. Gradually the theory evolved that each atom, far from being the smallest particle possible, is really like a tiny solar system, with a central "sun" or nucleus, which is made up of positively charged protons and neutral neutrons. Around this nucleus revolve many negative electrons, which balance the positive charge of the protons. The nucleus, it seems, is the controlling power of the atom. Change the nucleus and you change the atom. The catch is that the protons and neutrons of most atoms' nuclei stick together as if fastened with some cosmic glue, and firmly resist man's efforts to separate them.

The discovery of the true nature of the atom was prerequisite to the development of atomic bombs. So, too, was the discovery of radio-activity, in 1897, by Henry Becquerel. Radio-activity is the spontaneous release of atomic energy by certain heavy substances as they change into other substances. Radium is the most widely known of these, and its atomic energy has been used for years in the treatment of cancer. Scientists reasoned that if some elements thus spontaneously give up atomic energy in changing their nature, other elements could be artificially made to do the same.

The third basic discovery mentioned above, that mass and energy are the same thing in different states, and that mass can be converted into energy, was announced by Einstein in 1905. At first glance that seems to have no connection with the atomic bomb. But actually it completed the foundation on which the coming atomic age will rest. Men now realized that atoms can be split, that in the process energy is released, and that this energy can be mathematically computed in advance. All that remained was to devise methods and tools for smashing atoms to best advantage.

The complete story of the A-bomb and the H-bomb would fill many books and concern a great many men and women. In a single chapter we can do little more than tell the story of one of these men: the man who made a tool which was indispensable in the research that culminated in the A-bomb. His tool was a sort of super-slingshot (the whirl-around type with which David killed Goliath) that simplified the process of dividing the "indivisible" atom, and eventually showed men how to follow the sun's method of fusing hydrogen atoms—without a trip to the sun.

One January evening in 1929, young Professor Ernest O. Lawrence sat in the University of California library reading reports of experiments in physics. During the evening he came across a paper written by a unknown German, R. Wideroe, on the behavior of ions in a magnetic field. Dutifully, Lawrence began to read. Suddenly, a diagram caught his attention—a diagram of a piece of apparatus the man had used. With two long vacuum tubes fastened together, Wideroe had managed to step up the speed of the electrified particles to twice the energy of the voltage he had used.

"H'm," pondered Lawrence. "That's interesting. A small voltage can increase the speed of electrified atoms if it is applied to them repeatedly at the right time."

Like all physicists of the time, Lawrence knew that one of the barriers in the path of atom-smashing was the fact that tremendous voltages were necessary to work up sufficient speed to make the infinitesimal "bullets" powerful enough to crack an atom-nucleus.

Again he looked at the drawing. "Only two long vacuum tubes," his thoughts went on. "I wonder—if this Wideroe had used *ten* tubes, wouldn't he have increased the force of his atoms enormously? Great force with comparatively little voltage. That's what we need to crack atoms. I wonder...."

Lawrence never finished reading Wideroe's article. His mind was busy with the idea the diagram had suggested—an idea for a new tool for science.

Almost at once he discarded the notion of ten tubes in a line. Such an apparatus would be too long to be practical. He settled, instead, on a circular vacuum chamber between the poles of an electromagnet. With alternating current, he would whirl electrified particles in this chamber, bending them by means of the magnet. The same small voltage, used again and again, would give the particles a series of electrical kicks which would make them go faster and faster, in ever-widening circles, until they would shoot out through a slit in the side of the chamber. Thus he would have, he hoped, a sort of magnetic and electric slingshot which, while using relatively low voltages, could build up sufficiently high speeds in his projectiles to smash atoms.

With the help of a graduate student, Niels Edlefsen, Professor Lawrence built his first magnetic resonance accelerator, as he called his machine. The vacuum chamber was only four inches in diameter. Merely a toy, it seemed. But it worked. When they held a magnet at right angles to it and turned on the oscillating current, particles really did whirl around in bigger and bigger circles at increasing speed.

The two young physicists were pleased with their accomplishment. The little machine created a great deal of interest in the Physics Department of the University of California, and was soon nicknamed "cyclotron" because of the resemblance of its action to a small cyclone. In the next two years, Lawrence and his student assistants built another, and yet another small cyclotron. Each one worked better than its predecessor.

But Lawrence was still not satisfied. "If only," he said to the graduate students who were helping him, "If only we could get a bigger magnet—a really powerful one. Then we could build a real cyclotron. We might make one that could smash atoms."

"Yes," agreed a student ruefully. "But that would take an awfully big magnet. Where on earth could we find one?"

Lawrence shook his head. He had no idea.

A few days later, Dr. Leonard Fuller, head of the department of Electrical Engineering at the University of California, stopped to talk to Lawrence on the campus in Berkeley.

"I hear you want a big magnet," said Dr. Fuller.

"Yes." Lawrence nodded. "I certainly would like to have one. If I could make a cyclotron big enough. . . ."

Fuller interrupted. "How would you like a 65-ton magnet?"

Ernest Lawrence laughed. "Sure! I might as well wish for a 65-ton magnet as a 30-ton one. Both are out of the question."

"I can get you a 65-ton magnet if you want it," answered the other quickly.

Lawrence looked suspiciously at Fuller. Was this his idea of a joke?

"I'm serious," Fuller assured him with a smile, seeing the incredulity in the young professor's eyes. "I know where there's a huge magnet you can have. You know," he went on," besides my work here at the university, I'm vice-president of the Federal Telegraph Company. During the war we built four 65-ton magnets for round-the-world radio transmission. One of them was for China, but the war ended in 1918 before it could be shipped."

"Where is it now?" asked Lawrence eagerly.

"In Palo Alto. Been there ever since, just lying around."

"Well!" Lawrence's eyes were snapping with excitement behind his glasses. "What are we waiting for? My car's out here. Let's go down to Palo Alto!"

When the 65-ton magnet was installed in the Radiation Laboratory at Berkeley, Lawrence and his crew set to work to build the cyclotron of his dreams. It was an immense task. A trying and dangerous time. One difficulty after another was surmounted, only to be replaced by yet another. But at last it was finished. And it proved, indeed, the atom-smasher Lawrence had hoped for.

Between the poles of the huge magnet, but not otherwise connected with it, they had installed a circular vacuum chamber, with D-shaped electrodes which were attached to the cyclotron's powerhouse. Outside the exit of the chamber a target was set up, smeared with lithium 7 isotope, whose atoms they hoped to crack.

Into the center of the cyclotron they admitted a stream of atoms. (Heavy water hydrogen atoms were later found to work best.) After the negative electrons were stripped off the atoms by an arc from a tungsten filament, the remaining nuclei were caught up by the voltage. As the nuclei started out in a straight line, the electromagnet pulled them back, making them curve into an arc. Half-way round, the voltage reversed and pushed them on, the magnet again pulling them into a curve. This kept on and on, the nuclei picking up speed at each half-turn, and swinging in wider and wider circles. As the particles reached the outer edge of the cyclotron, they were traveling thousands of times faster than a bullet can go. Then out through the exit slit in the side of the chamber they shot, toward the target. And some of the speeding particles found their mark and cracked the nuclei of some of the lithium atoms. To their amazement and joy, Lawrence and his assistants found that they had broken the lithium atoms into two alpha particles.

That was in the summer of 1932. It was, of course, just the beginning. Ernest Lawrence not only went on working and experimenting with his atom-smasher, and building new and vastly bigger ones, but he trained other men in the work, and helped with the building of cyclotrons in other places.

Thus, when the United States was ready to begin intensive work on the problem of releasing atomic energy for use as a weapon of war, Ernest Lawrence and his efficient cyclotron were prepared to do their share toward the development of the atomic bomb, by producing U-235 in quantity, pure enough to be used in the making of the bombs.

Even before the first A-bomb was tested—before anybody knew whether it would work—scientists realized from their experimental work on it that its explosion would generate heat such as had never been known on this earth, and would build up tremendous pressure. The explosion of an atomic bomb, if it worked out as expected, would build up high enough pressure so that atoms would be close enough together for fusion to occur, and would generate a 50,000,000-degree temperature—more than twice as hot as inside the sun! And *that* heat could be used as the fuse to light a hydrogen-fusion bomb!

The A-bomb, which is fundamentally a chain-reaction of atom-smashing in a lump of pure U-235 (or plutonium, a product of U-235), lived up to expectations. And hydrogen-fusion moved up from theory to possibility, although there were still many difficulties in the way.

Chief of these difficulties was the time element. The A-bomb produced the heat required to set off the hydrogen-into-helium fusion of the H-bomb, but that heat lasted only a millionth of a second. So the search was on for materials that could be ignited in that incredibly brief space of time.

Hydrogen seemed best. Not the normal hydrogen, which is the most abundant element in the universe, but the heavier forms: deuterium (twice as heavy) and tritium (three times as heavy as normal hydrogen). The drawback of deuterium was that it takes far longer than a millionth of a second to start the fusion process at the 50,-000,000-degree temperature produced by the A-bomb; the match or fuse would burn out before the firecracker was lighted. The objection to tritium was that it is prohibitively expensive to make.*

* See "The Hell Bomb," by William L. Lawrence.

Eventually scientists found that a combination of the two—a lot of deuterium and a very little tritium—would produce the desired results, and the sun's method of producing energy (by hydrogen-into-helium fusion) became possible, with the A-bomb providing the sun's heat on the earth.

The End

General Bibliography

BOOKS

Am. Tel. and Tel. Co.: *The Telephone in America*
Bachman: *Great Inventors and Their Inventions*
Beard: *Our Foreign-Born Citizens*
Bridges: *Young Folks' Book of Invention*
Burlingame: *Engines of Democracy*
Carneal: *Conqueror of Space*
Corbin: *Marvels of Scientific Invention*
Darrow: *Builders of Empire*
       Boys' Own Book of Invention
       Masters of Science and Invention
Faris: *Men Who Conquered*
Holland: *Historic Inventions*
Hutchinson: *Easy Lessons in Television*
Hylander: *American Inventors*
Iles: *Leading American Inventors*
Kaempffert: *Modern Wonder Workers*
         Popular History of American Invention
Kerby: *Victory of Television*
Leeming: *Peaks of Invention*
Mackenzie: *Alexander Graham Bell*
Mills: *The Magic of Communication*
     Through Electrical Eyes
     Signals and Speech in Electrical Communication
Molloy: *The Link Trainer*
Morgan: *Pageant of Electricity*
Mullen: *This New Age*

THE STORY BEHIND GREAT INVENTIONS

Parkman: *Conquests of Invention*
Patterson: *America's Greatest Inventors*
Porterfield and Reynolds: *We Present Television*
Raborg: *Mechanized Might*
Rhodes: *Beginning of Telephony*
Thomas: *Magic Dials*
Towers: *From Beacon Fire to Radio*
University of Knowledge Wonder Books:
    Great Inventors and Their Inventions
    Amazing Facts in a Marvelous World
    Mysteries of Physics and Chemistry
War Dept.: *Link Trainer, Operation and Training*
Wile: *Emile Berliner*
Zworykin: *Photocells and Their Application*

Also

Drake's Cyclopedia of Radio and Electrons
Standard American Encyclopedia
Standard Handbook for the Electrical Engineer
Encyclopaedia Britannica and the Britannica Research Bureau

References for Revised Edition

The Hell Bomb, by William L. Lawrence, Knopf, 1950
How to Make an Atomic Bomb in Your Own Kitchen, by Bob Bale, Frederick Fell, 1951